Simply Vegetarian!

More than 80,000 sold !

WHAT OTHERS HAVE SAID ABOUT
Simply Vegetarian!

"*Simply Vegetarian!* is really outstanding!"
—"A.M. LOS ANGELES"

"Recipe after recipe for people who just like good food."
—KCBS RADIO, SAN FRANCISCO

"**Simply Vegetarian!** is practical and helpful, and deserves daily use in anyone's kitchen."
—VEGETARIAN JOURNAL

"In this age of greater awareness about the dangers of a meat-based diet, **Simply Vegetarian!** is ideal for non-vegetarians as well as vegetarians, and it is especially appropriate for those making the transition into vegetarianism."
—THE BOOKWATCH

"**Simply Vegetarian!** makes you rethink the idea that vegetarian food is blah! Fact of the matter is you don't have to be a vegetarian to enjoy this book."
—RENO GAZETTE-JOURNAL

"**Simply Vegetarian!** does not demand 'health-nut' status of its cooks."
—THE REGINA LEADER-POST

"Move over Moosewood. **Simply Vegetarian!** is bound to be a strong competitor."
—THE RIVERSIDE PRESS-ENTERPRISE

Simply Vegetarian!

EASY-TO-PREPARE RECIPES FOR THE VEGETARIAN GOURMET

DAWN Publications
14618 Tyler Foote Road   Nevada City, California 95959

Libray of Congress Cataloging-in-Publication Data
Simply vegetarian! : easy-to-prepare recipes
for the vegetarian gourmet
Rev. ed. — Nevada City, Calif. : Crystal Clarity, 1989.
249 p. : ill. ; 23cm.
Rev. ed. editors: Nancy Mair, Susan Rinzler.
Rev. ed. of : The Ananda cookbook.
ISBN 0-916124-53-3 : $11.95
1. Vegetarian cookery. I. Title: Ananda cookbook.
TX837.S49 1989   641.5'636 90-131641

Printed on recycled paper using vegetable based ink
Printed in Canada

16 15 14 13 12 11 10 9

Contents

Acknowledgements

THIS COOKBOOK is the product of many hands and hearts. We would like to thank all those who helped to create it, especially the many people at Ananda who shared their favorite recipes. Special thanks are due a number of people: Christine Ross and Nancy Mair for their dedication (and endurance!) in testing and retesting hundreds of recipes, and for their invaluable editorial assistance; Janice Boldt for the basic cover and page design; Julia Beinhorn, Martin Benkler, and Bella Potapovsky for their long hours of design work; Maria Potapovsky for typing hundreds of recipes; Dorothy Levit and Lynn Miller for typing the final manuscript; Patricia Black for her work on the index; George Beinhorn for his indispensable advice and assistance with tele-typesetting; Fern Lucki for helping to launch the project; David Praver for his support and confidence that the cookbook would indeed someday be ready; Garth Gilchrist and Joseph Okpaku for their patience and support; and J. Donald Walters for his guiding inspiration.

Asha Praver and Sheila Rush
Cookbook Editors

Introduction to the First Edition

HAVE YOU EVER WONDERED why so many people claim that "Mom's cooking is best" and why, even if you follow her recipe, it just doesn't turn out the same? A good recipe is a starting point, but cooking well is more than a matter of technique. There are many intangibles which make the difference in how a meal tastes—your thoughts, your attitudes, your consciousness while you work. *You, in fact, are the most important ingredient in any recipe.* Food takes on the quality of the person preparing it, and if there is a special relationship between that person and the one being served—the food will show it. The old saying, "the way to a man's heart is through his stomach," contains more subtle truth than many people realize. Food, when prepared with love, satisfies more than the physical appetite. It nurtures on many levels.

Sound like a heavy responsibility? It really isn't. The best way to do it right is simply to have fun cooking. Just as your philodendron responds to your cheerful words and loving vibrations, so also do the carrots and the rice and the Italian salad dressing. They like to be treated kindly, with respect for what they have to offer. They will give more to you if you give more to them. Even if you are only slicing an apple—pay attention. Do it carefully, lovingly, as well as you can. Enjoy the process as well as the results and the results will be much more delicious.

Introduction to the Revised Edition

WHEN WE DECIDED to revise the original cookbook, we did so only to make a good thing better. The first edition, **The Ananda Cookbook**, has enjoyed four years of success including two years in a row as a book-of-the-month club selection.

But just as a good cook tinkers with a recipe in search of perfection, we decided to update the cookbook offerings to reflect current trends, both vegetarian and mainstream. **Simply Vegetarian!** is the delightful result. New recipes add to the original sparkle without sacrificing our original goal: a cuisine that appeals to both vegetarians and non-vegetarians.

Vegetarians in search of meals of superior taste will be pleased to include our recipes in their repertoire of fine vegetarian cooking. Non-vegetarians who are moving in the direction of healthier, more balanced diets, will be more than reassured to find that taste and texture combine with imagination to make meatless meals that are a pleasure.

There is no pretence about this cookbook. It does what it says it does by providing complete gourmet meals that are easy to prepare. In fact, we went out of our way to maintain a middle ground of reasonable preparation time. Many of our dishes take 30 minutes or less to prepare. The ingredients are easy to find in your local market, and clear, easy-to-follow directions include preparation time and number of servings.

Simply Vegetarian! comes to you from our community of vegetarians in northern California, our vegetarian restaurant, catering service and retreat center which specializes in vegetarian meals for guests from all over the world. It is the distillation of years of experience putting together meals with loving hearts and hands. In this spirit, we offer you dishes that are simply delicious as well as simply vegetarian.

Nancy Mair
Susan Rinzler
Revised Edition Editors

A Note on Preparation Time

BY "PREPARATION TIME" we mean the time you are *actively* preparing the dish—sautéeing, chopping, stirring, blending, etc. Preparation time includes cooking time unless the dish cooks or bakes unattended for a long period, leaving you free to do other things. Where this is the case, we have listed cooking and preparation times separately.

Please note that all such times are averages which will vary from person to person, depending on experience.

Recipes

Soups

Vichyssoise

Preparation time: 40-45 minutes

Sauté in large saucepan over medium heat until tender:
6 tablespoons butter
5 medium leeks, minced (white part only)
1 medium-large onion, minced

Add, cover, and simmer for 15 minutes or until potatoes are tender:
4 cups vegetable broth (dissolve 4 unsalted vegetable bouillon cubes in 4 cups boiling water)
4 medium potatoes, cubed

Reserve 3 cups of soup and purée the rest in blender until smooth. Return to saucepan and add:
3 tablespoons chopped fresh chives
salt, to taste
⅛ teaspoon black pepper or, to taste

Heat gently, stirring constantly until mixture comes to a boil. Serve at once.

Spinach-Herb Soup

Serves: 4-6

An excellent luncheon or first course dish.

Preparation time: 45-50 minutes

Sauté in heavy saucepan over medium heat until spinach and celery are wilted:

½ cup butter
4 rounded tablespoons chopped fresh chives
4 cups (packed) chopped fresh spinach, leaves only
    (about 2 large bunches)
2 cups finely chopped celery
2 teaspoons tarragon

Add:

6 cups water
8 salted vegetable bouillon cubes (Vegex brand tends
    to work best for this recipe)
1 teaspoon honey
¾ teaspoon garlic powder

Bring mixture to a boil, reduce heat, then simmer for 15 minutes. Purée mixture in blender until smooth. Serve garnished with any one or more of the following:

sour cream or yogurt
finely chopped fresh chives
slice of lemon
paprika

Bella's Borscht

Serves: 6-8 large servings

Preparation time: 30 minutes
Cooking time: 1 hour and 15 minutes. The longer it cooks, the better it
gets!

Place in large soup pot and bring to a boil:

> **10 cups water**
> **4 cups diced beets**
> **4½ cups shredded cabbage**
> **2 cups sliced carrots**
> **3 cups chopped onions**
> **1½ cups diced potatoes**
> **1 small-medium bay leaf**
> **¾ teaspoon garlic powder**
> **scant ½ teaspoon dried dill weed**
> **1 rounded teaspoon salt**
> **scant teaspoon black pepper**

Reduce heat to simmer and cook covered for 45 minutes.
Serve with:

> **dollop of sour cream and chopped chives**

Cucumber-Yogurt Soup

Serves: 3-4

Preparation time: 15 minutes
Chilling time: 1 hour

Peel and grate:

2 large cucumbers

Blend in blender with grated cucumbers (in two batches):

4 cups yogurt
2 tablespoons olive oil
1½ tablespoons white wine vinegar
2 small garlic cloves, crushed
¾ teaspoon chopped fresh mint
⅛ teaspoon salt

Chill for 1 hour. Serve garnished with:

chopped fresh parsley

Oriental Miso Soup

Serves: 4 large servings

A fresh, full-bodied flavor.

Preparation time: 20 minutes
Cooking time: 5 minutes

Bring to a boil, then simmer for 5 minutes:
1 quart water
10 thin slices fresh ginger root (be sure to peel
before slicing)
2 cups peas, fresh or frozen
Scant $^1/_8$ teaspoon cayenne pepper
Scant $^1/_4$ teaspoon cumin powder
4 cloves garlic, minced or pressed

Add:
1$^1/_4$ cups tomato juice

Remove from heat, cool slightly, then add, first mix
ing with a little hot broth to liquify miso*:
$^1/_2$ cup yellow or light miso

Remove ginger slices** and serve.

Please note:

*Don't boil after adding miso. The high heat destroys
miso's living enzymes.

**If ginger slices sit in soup too long after adding
miso, the flavor will become too strong.

Hearty Miso-Onion Soup

Serves: 4

If you like French Onion Soup . . .

Preparation time: 25-30 minutes

Sauté in large saucepan over medium heat until onions are soft:

6 tablespoons butter
1½ large red onions, thinly sliced
1½ cups (packed) sliced mushrooms

Add:

3¾ cups water

Bring to a boil, then reduce heat. Stir in, first mixing with a little hot broth to liquify miso*:

5-6 tablespoons red miso

Add:

6 tablespoons freshly grated Parmesan cheese

Season with:

3 tablespoons minced fresh parsley
⅛ teaspoon black pepper

Please note:

*Don't boil after adding miso. The high heat destroys miso's living enzymes.

Gazpacho

Serves: 6-8

Refreshing and energizing. Lovely on a hot summer day.

Preparation time: 30 minutes
Chilling time: several hours

Combine in large bowl:

1 large can (46 ounces) tomato juice
2 cucumbers, peeled and diced
2 green bell peppers, diced
2 tomatoes, chopped
5-6 tablespoons lemon juice (2 lemons)
2 large cloves garlic, minced
2 tablespoons finely chopped parsley or fresh
cilantro — or more to taste.
2 tablespoons olive oil
1/4-1/2 teaspoon cumin powder
salt, to taste
1/8-1/4 teaspoon black pepper

Chill for several hours. Serve ice cold.

optional: **tabasco**
                diced avocado
                sliced olives

Tomato Soup

Serves: 4-6

Light and fresh-tasting.

Preparation time: 20-25 minutes
Cooking time: 1 hour

Sauté in large saucepan over medium heat:
3 tablespoons olive oil
1 large onion, chopped
1 large green bell pepper, chopped
3 cloves garlic, minced

Add:
3 cups tomato juice
3 cups peeled, seeded and chopped fresh tomatoes
1 salted vegetable bouillon cube
1½ teaspoons dried dill weed
1½ teaspoons basil
1 teaspoon dried parsley
⅛ teaspoon black pepper

Cover and cook over low heat for about 1 hour. Stir in:
1 teaspoon honey

Variation:
During last hour of cooking, add:
1 cup cubed raw potatoes

Cream of Asparagus Soup

Serves: 4

Wonderfully flavorful.

Preparation time: 35 minutes
Cooking time: 30 minutes

Remove any tough ends and cut into ¹/₂-inch pieces
(reserving the tips):
  2 pounds asparagus

Melt in a large pot:
  6 tablespoons unsalted butter

Add and sauté, stirring frequently until tender:
  ³/₄ cup chopped green onion

Add asparagus (except tips) to pan. Sauté lightly for a
few minutes, stirring frequently. Now add and bring

to a boil:
   8 cups water
   2 vegetable buillon cubes, (1 salted, 1 unsalted)

Reduce heat and cover pan. Simmer for 20 minutes, or until asparagus is tender. Blend the soup and return it to the pan. Add the reserved asparagus tips and simmer for 5 to 10 minutes, just until they are done.

To serve hot, garnish each bowl with a dollop of:
   crème fraîche or sour cream

To serve chilled, add to the pot of soup:
   $^1/_2$ cup cream

Creamy Broccoli-Leek Soup   Serves: 6-8

Preparation time: 35 minutes

In a large saucepan, sauté over medium heat for about 8 minutes:

1 cube butter (½ cup)
8 cups (packed) trimmed and coarsely chopped broccoli (approximately 2 pounds)
1½ cups sliced leeks (use white and light-green parts only)
1 medium-large potato, cubed

Add:

8 cups vegetable broth (dissolve 2 salted and 2 unsalted vegetable bouillon cubes in 8 cups boiling water)

Bring to a boil, lower heat and cook for 15-20 minutes or until tender. Reserve ½ cup broccoli florets for garnish. Purée mixture in blender in batches until smooth. Return to saucepan and add:

black pepper, to taste

Heat through. Serve garnished with reserved broccoli. You might like to add:

dollop of sour cream sprinkled with paprika

Broccoli Bisque

Serves: 7-8

Very rich.

Preparation time: 30 minutes
Cooking time: 25 minutes

Sauté in large saucepan over medium heat until tender:
4 tablespoons butter
¾ cup thinly sliced yellow onions
¼ cup chopped green onions
1 cup sliced mushrooms

Add and stir until bubbling:
¼ cup whole wheat pastry flour

Remove from heat and gradually whisk in:
3 cups vegetable broth (dissolve 1½ salted vegetable bouillon cubes in 3 cups boiling water)

Return to heat and stir until thickened and smooth.
Add:
1 cup broccoli florets (if large, split into smaller pieces)

Reduce heat and simmer for 20 minutes or until vegetables are tender. Add:
½ cup half and half
½ cup milk
2 cups grated Swiss cheese

Simmer until heated throughout and cheese is melted.

Variation:
For an extra-rich soup eliminate milk and use:
1 cup half and half

Potato-Cheese Soup

Serves: 4-6

A thick chowder-like soup.

Preparation time: 35 minutes

Boil until tender in large saucepan:
4 cups sliced potatoes
**4 cups vegetable broth (dissolve 1½-2 unsalted vege-
    table bouillon cubes in 4 cups boiling water)**
salt, to taste

Meanwhile, sauté until soft, then add to vegetable broth:
2 tablespoons butter
2 large celery stalks, finely chopped
1 medium onion, diced

Purée above ingredients in blender with:
1 tablespoon minced fresh parsley or more, to taste

Pour blended mixture into saucepan, reheat, and add:
3 cups milk
1 cup (packed) grated sharp cheddar cheese
1 teaspoon basil
½ teaspoon garlic powder
¼ teaspoon black pepper

Heat until cheese melts and flavors are well-blended—
about 5 to 10 minutes.

Czech Mushroom Soup

Very rich.

Preparation time: 20 minutes
Cooking time: 20 minutes

Boil in large covered saucepan for 15 minutes:
4 cups water
4 medium-large potatoes*, diced
2 teaspoons salt
1 teaspoon caraway seeds

Reduce heat, mix together and stir into soup:
¼ cup whole wheat pastry flour
2 pints sour cream

Add and simmer (covered) for 10 minutes, stirring occasionally to prevent sticking:
1 pound sliced mushrooms

Remove from heat. Before serving, sprinkle with:
**1 teaspoon dried dill weed or 1 tablespoon minced
    fresh dill**

Variation:

For a less rich soup, use:
1 pint milk
1 pint sour cream

Please note:

*We prefer unpeeled potatoes. Peeled potatoes will give
you a slightly smoother, more delicate flavor.

Deluxe Pea Soup with Curry

Cooking time: 25-30 minutes
Preparation time: 20 minutes
Yields: 1 quart

In a large pot, cook until soft; about 20-25 minutes.
Add more water if necessary:
**1 cup of lentils or yellow split peas or green
    split peas
3 cups water
1 teaspoon salt**

Salads

Greek Salad

Serves: 6-8 generously

Traditionally served with a black bread.

Preparation time: 30 minutes
(Including dressing)

Wash and dry the leaves of:
  1 large head Romaine lettuce, or 2 small heads

Tear the lettuce into bite-sized pieces. Layer in a large salad bowl along with:
  3 large tomatoes, cut in wedges, then in half
  1-2 cucumbers, sliced or cubed
  ¹/₂ of a purple onion or to taste, thinly sliced, then quartered
  1 green bell pepper, thinly sliced, then cut into thirds

Garnish the top with:
  ³/₄-1 pound feta cheese
  10 ounces Greek olives (Kalamata)

Serve with **Greek Salad Dressing.**

Mix in a blender:
  ³/₄ cup olive oil
  ¹/₄ cup red wine vinegar
  3 tablespoons fresh lemon juice
  3 cloves garlic, chopped
  1¹/₄ teaspoons oregano
  ¹/₄ teaspoon dill
  1 teaspoon salt
  black pepper, to taste

Rainbow Salad

Serves: 8-12

A meal in itself.

Preparation time: 45-50 minutes
Chilling time: overnight

Place in layers in large glass bowl:
2 medium heads iceberg lettuce, coarsely chopped
1 cup chopped green onions
one 8-ounce can water chestnuts, drained and sliced
**1 small package frozen petite peas, thawed and un-
    cooked**
½ cup freshly grated Parmesan cheese
1 cup chopped celery

Cover the above with mixture of:
1 cup mayonnaise
1 cup sour cream
1 cup herb salad dressing (page 61)

Chill overnight. Then add next three layers of:
5 hard-boiled eggs, chopped
enough tomato slices to cover top layer
1 cup vegetarian baco bits (optional)

Serve garnished with:
chopped ripe black olives

Great for picnics, parties, brunches, etc.

Raw Vegetable Salad

Serves: 2-4

Preparation time: 20 minutes

Combine in large bowl:

1½ cups grated carrots
1 tomato, chopped
1 avocado, chopped
½ cup grated beets (peel large or tough-skinned beets
    before grating)
2 tablespoons-¼ cup sunflower seeds

Mix together and pour over vegetables (you may not want to use all of the dressing):

¾ cup light vegetable oil
2 tablespoons red wine vinegar
1 teaspoon tamari
¾ teaspoon nutritional yeast
1¼ teaspoons molasses
⅛ teaspoon Vegit (available at health food stores)
⅛ teaspoon garlic powder
⅛ teaspoon onion powder

Serve on a bed of lettuce.

Jicama Salad

Preparation time: 25 minutes
Soaking time: 2 hours

Soak covered in slightly salted water for 2 hours:
1 medium red onion, thinly sliced into rounds

Blend together:
3 tablespoons fresh lemon juice or more, to taste
1½ tablespoons lime juice or more, to taste
1½ teaspoons grated lemon peel
pinch of salt
black pepper, to taste

Slowly whisk in:
6 tablespoons peanut oil
¾ cup olive oil
1 tablespoon minced fresh parsley

In a large bowl, place:
1½-1¾ pounds jicama, peeled and cut into
matchstick julienne

Add vinaigrette to jicama and toss. Drain, pat dry, and stir in onion rings. On a platter, arrange:
red leaf lettuce leaves

Place jicama and onion on top of lettuce. Garnish with:
cherry tomatoes
green bell pepper rings

Serve immediately.

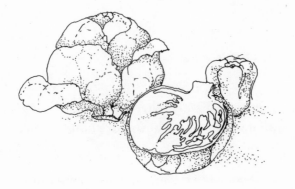

Cole Slaw

Serves: 6

Preparation time: 10-15 minutes
Chilling time: several hours

Mix together:

4 cups grated or shredded green cabbage
1 medium carrot, grated
½ cup mayonnaise
2 tablespoons lemon juice
scant tablespoon grated onion
½ teaspoon salt
⅛ teaspoon black pepper
1 tablespoon poppy seeds
1 teaspoon honey (optional)

This salad tastes best when refrigerated for several hours to allow flavors to blend.

Variation:

Add:

½ cup finely chopped green bell pepper

For a more colorful salad, use purple cabbage.

Carrot Salad

Serves: 4

Preparation time: 10 minutes
Chilling time: 45 minutes

Mix together in large bowl:

3 cups shredded carrots (about 3 large carrots)
¼ cup raisins
1-1½ teaspoons lemon juice
1 tablespoon honey (add another ½ teaspoon if
carrots aren't very sweet)
½ cup mayonnaise

Chill and serve.

Variations:

1. Instead of mayonnaise, use:

½ cup yogurt

Omit lemon juice and add:

2 tablespoons chopped cashews

2. For a more substantial salad, add to basic recipe:

½ cup grated Jack or cheddar cheese
2 tablespoons chopped cashews

Tomato-Mushroom Salad with Marinade

Serves: 8

Preparation time: 25 minutes
Chilling time: several hours

To make marinade, blend in blender:

1¼ cups olive oil
2 tablespoons lemon juice
6 tablespoons red wine vinegar
4 large or 8 small cloves garlic
1½ teaspoons basil
¼ teaspoon black pepper
2 teaspoons chopped fresh parsley
1 tablespoon plus 1 teaspoon Worcestershire sauce
1 tablespoon plus 1 teaspoon dry mustard
1 teaspoon honey

Pour marinade over:

1 bunch green onions (about 7) including tops, sliced very thin
5 large tomatoes, cut into eighths (then sliced crossways if desired)
10 cups button mushrooms, quartered

Mix well and refrigerate for several hours. Stir occasionally.

Beet Salad

Serves: 5-6

Light and flavorful.

Preparation time: 20 minutes
Cooking time: 20-25 minutes

In a large bowl, mix together:

⅓ cup mayonnaise
1 tablespoon lemon juice
scant teaspoon salt

Add:

4 cups diced cooked beets
2 tablespoons finely chopped chives or green onions
1 tablespoon chopped fresh parsley

Mix well and taste. Add more salt and/or lemon juice if needed. This dish keeps well in the refrigerator and can be prepared in advance.

French Vegetable Salad

Serves: 8-10

A decorative luncheon dish.

Preparation time: 30-35 minutes

Peel, cut into quarters, and steam until crisp-tender:

4 small beets (about 10 ounces)

Rinse cooked beets under cold water and pat dry. While beets are cooking, coarsely grate:

2 medium zucchini
2 medium carrots

Steam for several minutes until crisp-tender:

one 20-ounce package frozen French green beans

Line a serving platter with red leaf or bibb lettuce leaves. Mound green beans in center. Encircle the beans with grated carrots, then with zucchini. Add in whatever decorative pattern you choose:

1 basket cherry tomatoes
one 5¾-ounce can black olives, drained

Then add quartered beets. Garnish with:

raw sunflower seeds
chopped fresh chives

Serve with your favorite French dressing.

French Potato Salad

Serves: 8-10

A *tangy, marinated version.*

Preparation time: 30 minutes
Chilling time: 30 minutes

Boil in skins until done but not mushy:
10 large potatoes

While potatoes cook, blend in blender:
½ cup vegetable oil
½ cup apple cider vinegar
3 teaspoons salt
¾ teaspoon black pepper
1 tablespoon dry mustard
1½ teaspoons basil
1½ teaspoons thyme
1½ teaspoons dried dill weed or more, to taste
1½ teaspoons tarragon
2 large cloves garlic
1 tablespoon honey

Cut warm potatoes, peeled or unpeeled, into dressing.
Mix well and chill. Add:
**¼ cup minced green onions (including tops) or more,
      to taste**
1½ cups mayonnaise
chopped celery, to taste (optional)

Garnish as desired with any one or more of the following:
black or pimiento-stuffed green olives
parsley
chopped chives

Hot German Potato Salad

Serves: 4-5

Preparation time: 35-40 minutes

Boil in skins until done:
7 medium-large potatoes cut in fourths, lengthwise

Meanwhile, cook according to package instructions:
one 5-ounce package of Stripples

Remove Stripples' from skillet with slotted spoon and drain on a paper towel. Sauté in same skillet using leftover oil until onions are transparent:
1¼ cups chopped onions
½ teaspoon caraway seeds
¾ cup chopped celery
1½ teaspoons dill weed
1 teaspoon crushed tarragon

Add crumbled, cooked Stripples. In a separate skillet, bring to a boil and add to sautéed mixture:
2 teaspoons honey
⅜ cup water
¾ cup apple cider vinegar or more, to taste
¼ teaspoon paprika
½ teaspoon dry mustard

Dice the cooked potatoes and add to the sautéed mixture. Add:
salt and pepper, to taste

Serve with:
chopped fresh parsley or chives

Country-Style Potato Salad

Serves: 4

Preparation time: 15 minutes
Cooking time: 20-30 minutes
Chilling time: 30 minutes

Boil until tender:

4 large white potatoes, diced

Meanwhile, hard boil:

2 eggs

While potatoes are still warm add and mix well:

1 tablespoon apple cider vinegar
½ teaspoon garlic powder
⅛-¼ teaspoon salt
¼ teaspoon beau monde or celery salt
¼ cup minced red or yellow onions
pinch of dry mustard

Let cool. Add and mix well:

1 tablespoon light vegetable oil
¼ cup plus 2 tablespoons mayonnaise
2 hard-boiled eggs, chopped

Sprinkle lightly with:

paprika

Variation:

For a slightly different taste, add:

¼ teaspoon dried dill weed
¼ cup chopped celery

Mexican Salad

A meal in itself—one of our favorites.

Preparation time: 25 minutes
Cooking time for rice: 45 minutes
Chilling time: 30 minutes

Sauté for 5 minutes in medium skillet:

1½ tablespoons butter
1½ cups cooked rice
scant ½ teaspoon chile powder
⅛ teaspoon coriander
scant ½ teaspoon cumin powder
½ teaspoon garlic powder
¼ teaspoon paprika

Allow to cool. In a large bowl, mix the above with:

1½ cups cooked kidney beans (canned work fine)
1 head iceberg lettuce, cut into bite-size pieces
¼-½ cup minced yellow or red onions
one 4-ounce can diced Ortega chiles
one 3½-5-ounce can pitted black olives, sliced

Then add:

3 tomatoes, diced
⅓ pound cheddar cheese, cut into small pieces

Top with:

¼ pound corn chips, broken into bite-size pieces

Chill and serve with Ranch Dressing (page 57). This salad goes well with corn bread.

Pasta Salad

Serves: 10-12

Great for picnics on a hot summer evening.
It keeps well for several days in the refrigerator.

Preparation time: 40 minutes

Place a large kettle of water on high heat. While
waiting for it to boil, prepare the dressing by blending
in the blender:

1 cup plus 2 tablespoons olive oil
the oil from 2 6-ounce jars of marinated artichoke
    hearts (They go in the salad later.)
³/₄ cup red wine vinegar
4¹/₂ tablespoons dried basil
4¹/₂ tablespoons chopped green onion
¹/₄ cup freshly grated Parmesan
1³/₄ teaspoons salt
¹/₄ teaspoon black pepper
3 tablespoons oregano

Cook in the boiling water, stirring occasionally until
tender (about 10 minutes):

2 pounds fusilli (corkscrew) or other shaped pasta
salt (¹/₂ tablespoon per quart of water)

Meanwhile, prepare and set aside:

1 large red bell pepper, chopped
1-2 green bell peppers, chopped
2 baskets cherry tomatoes *or* 3 large tomatoes,
    chopped
3 6-ounce jars marinated artichoke hearts (drain
    from oil and remove any tough outer leaves)
¹/₂ pound Jack cheese, cubed
1¹/₂-2 6-ounce cans black olives, halved
¹/₂ large cucumber, peeled and chopped

Drain the pasta when tender. Place in a very large
bowl. While still warm, add the dressing and bell
peppers. Stir. When cooled to room temperature, add
the remaining ingredients. Chill until ready to serve.

Tabouli

Serves: 8

Preparation time: 35-40 minutes
Soaking time: 1 hour
Chilling time: 1 hour

Combine, cover and soak for 1 hour
   4 cups boiling water
   2 cups dry bulgur wheat

Meanwhile, combine in large bowl:
   $^1/_2$ cup lemon juice
   **2-4 tablespoons minced fresh mint, or dried mint
   to taste**
   4 cloves of garlic, put through a garlic press
   2 teaspoons salt
   $^1/_2$ teaspoon black pepper

Whisk in slowly:
   $^1/_2$ cup olive oil

Stir in:
   **$1^1/_2$- 2 cups finely chopped parsley (about 2 large
   bunches)**
   $^3/_4$ cup chopped green onions (including tops)
   3 tomatoes, chopped
   1 cup peeled and diced cucumber

Mix together with soaked wheat and refrigerate for 1
hour before serving.

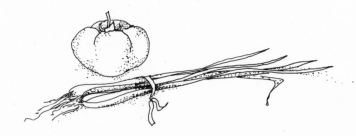

Summer Rice Salad

Serves: 6-8

Preparation time: 50 minutes (not including time for cooking rice)
Chilling time: 1 hour

Combine in large bowl:

**6 cups warm brown rice (you can use warmed
leftover rice or freshly cooked rice)
two 6-ounce jars marinated artichoke hearts,
chopped, including marinade
4 tablespoons red wine vinegar
3 tablespoons lemon juice
4 tablespoons olive oil
1½ teaspoons thyme or more, to taste
1¼ teaspoons garlic powder or more, to taste
2½ teaspoons basil
salt and black pepper, to taste
one 3-ounce jar pimiento-stuffed green olives,
drained and sliced
one large (about 6 ounces) can pitted black olives,
drained and sliced**

Chill the above. While mixture chills, prepare:

**1 cup chopped green bell peppers
2 cups peeled, seeded, and chopped cucumbers
6 large green onions, chopped (tops included)
4 large tomatoes, chopped
¾ cup finely chopped fresh parsley
1½ cups chopped celery**

After salad chills stir in an additional:

**4 tablespoons red wine vinegar
3 tablespoons olive oil**

Adjust seasoning if necessary. Serve on a bed of lettuce
leaves garnished with:

**cherry tomatoes
green bell pepper rings
olives**

Egg Salad

Serves: 2-3

Preparation time: 20 minutes

Coarsely chop:
6 hard-boiled eggs

Combine with eggs in large bowl and mix well:
3 tablespoons mayonnaise
¼ rounded teaspoon curry powder
¼ teaspoon cumin powder
⅛ teaspoon Spike (available at health food stores)
¼ teaspoon grey Poupon mustard
black pepper, to taste
2 tablespoons minced celery
salt, to taste

Egg Salad with Cashews

Serves: 3-4

Preparation time: 20 minutes

Coarsely chop:
1 dozen hard-boiled eggs

Combine with eggs in large bowl and mix well:
2 tablespoons wet mustard or more, to taste
½ cup plus 2 tablespoons mayonnaise
salt and black pepper, to taste
¼ teaspoon paprika
2 tablespoons minced fresh chives
½ cup finely chopped toasted cashews or more, to
  taste

Garnish with any of the following:
sliced avocado
sliced mushrooms
sprouts

Tofu Salad

Serves: 4

"Mock tuna salad".

Preparation time: 15 minutes

Mix together in large bowl:
1 pound tofu, drained, rinsed, and mashed
½ cup mayonnaise
4 tablespoons catsup
2-3 tablespoons tamari or, to taste
4 tablespoons nutritional yeast
1½-2 cups chopped celery
¼ teaspoon herb salt or Spike (available in health food stores)
1 teaspoon onion powder
½ teaspoon garlic powder

Serve with vegetable sticks, chips, or as a sandwich spread.

Variations:
1. For a spicier version add:
½ cup Picante sauce or more, to taste

2. Add to salad and adjust seasonings:
cooked elbow macaroni
mayonnaise

Apple-Celery Salad
with Banana Dressing

Serves: 3-5

Preparation time: 15 minutes

Combine in medium bowl and set aside:
   ¼-⅓ cup chopped dates (4 large dates)
   ½ cup chopped celery (1-2 stalks)
   2 large or 4 small diced green apples

Grind in blender:
   ¼ cup walnuts

Then add:
   2 ripe mashed bananas
   1 tablespoon honey
   1 tablespoon freshly squeezed lemon juice

Combine banana mixture with apples and celery. Top servings with:
   ⅓ cup chopped walnuts

Serve immediately. The banana dressing darkens quickly, although it will still taste fine.

Variation:
   Instead of dates, use:
      2 tablespoons raisins

Festive Cranberry Salad

Serves: 6-8

Preparation time: 20 minutes
Chilling time: 1-1½ hours

Boil in saucepan until skins pop:
12 ounces fresh cranberries
1 cup water

Add and let cool a bit:
½-¾ cup honey

Pour cranberry mixture into large bowl. Add and mix
well:
1 cup grated coconut
4 oranges, peeled, seeded, sectioned and diced
½ cup chopped walnuts

Chill and serve.

Salad Dressings

Tomato Juice
Salad Dressing

Makes: 1½ cups

Preparation time: 5-10 minutes

Blend in blender:
    1 cup thick tomato juice
    4 tablespoons safflower oil
    4 tablespoons apple cider vinegar
    ½ teaspoon basil
    3 cloves garlic
    ⅛ teaspoon freshly ground black pepper
    honey, to taste

Tangy Tomato Dressing

Makes: 1½ cups

Preparation time: 5 minutes

Blend in blender:
    ⅔ cup vegetable oil
    ⅓ cup catsup
    1½ tablespoons honey or more, to taste
    ⅓ cup red wine vinegar (we recommend
        garlic-flavored)
    2 teaspoons Worcestershire sauce

Toss salad with dressing. Add:
    salt and black pepper, to taste

Goes well with a spinach-raw mushroom salad.

Ranch Dressing

Makes: 2 cups

Preparation time: 10 minutes

Mix together or blend in blender:

$^1/_2$ cup mayonnaise
$^1/_2$ cup sour cream
1 cup buttermilk
1 tablespoon plus 1 teaspoon chopped chives *or* finely
    chopped green onions (tops only)
2 teaspoons parsley
$^1/_4$ teaspoon cumin powder
$^1/_4$ rounded teaspoon garlic powder
$^1/_4$ rounded teaspoon onion powder
small pinch of cayenne
dash of paprika
generous pinch of salt
generous pinch of black pepper

Refrigerate 1 hour or longer to allow flavors to blend
(optional).

Blue Cheese Dressing

Makes: 1$^1/_2$ cups

Preparation time: 5-10 minutes

Mix together or blend in blender:
$^1/_2$ cup sour cream
$^1/_2$ cup mayonnaise
$^1/_4$ cup buttermilk
$^1/_4$ teaspoon garlic powder
$^1/_8$ teaspoon onion powder
1-3 tablespoons blue cheese
pinch of cayenne

Creamy Italian Dressing

Makes: 2 cups

Preparation time: 5-8 minutes

Blend in blender:
⅓ cup water
¼ cup apple cider vinegar
1 tablespoon honey
1 egg
½ teaspoon celery seed
⅛ teaspoon dry mustard
1 large clove garlic
1 teaspoon savory
1 teaspoon tarragon
1 teaspoon salt
½ teaspoon black pepper

While blender is on, slowly add:
1 cup vegetable oil

Yogurt Salad Dressing

Makes: 2 cups

Preparation time: 5-8 minutes

Combine and mix well:
2 cups yogurt (thinned with milk if desired)
¾ teaspoon garlic powder
½ teaspoon onion powder
¾ teaspoon dried dill weed
¼ teaspoon beau monde or celery salt
¼ teaspoon paprika
½ teaspoon cumin powder
¼ teaspoon salt

Variations:

> Blend above mixture in blender with any of the following:
>
> **½ cup chopped cooked beets (do not thin yogurt)**
> **chopped fresh tomatoes, to taste (do not thin yogurt)**
> **mashed avocado, to taste**

Cassidy French Dressing   Makes: 1½ cups

Preparation time: 10 minutes

> Blend in blender:
> **¼-⅓ cup apple cider vinegar**
> **2 tablespoons Dijon prepared mustard**
> **1 tablespoon honey**
> **½ teaspoon salt**
>
> Slowly add and blend with rest of mixture:
> **1 cup olive oil**
>
> Add to above mixture:
> **2 cloves garlic, minced**
> **2 tablespoons chopped yellow or red onions**
> **¼ cup finely chopped fresh parsley (remove stems)**

Refrigerate for 1 hour to allow flavors to blend (optional).

Luscious Green Dressing

Makes: 2 cups

Slightly sweet yet tangy.

Preparation time: 10 minutes

Blend in blender:
1 cup safflower or olive oil
½ cup apple cider vinegar
1 cup chopped fresh parsley (remove stems)
1 small green onion, chopped
2 tablespoons peeled and grated ginger root
⅓ cup honey
⅛ teaspoon basil
¼ rounded teaspoon curry powder
¼ teaspoon dry mustard
⅛ teaspoon salt
pinch of black pepper

Herb Salad Dressing

Makes: 2¼ cups

Rich, pungent taste.

Preparation time: 5 minutes

Blend in blender:
   1¼ cups vegetable oil
   ⅓-½ cup apple cider vinegar
   ¼ cup lemon juice
   1 tablespoon tamari
   1 teaspoon garlic powder
   ½ teaspoon oregano
   ¼ teaspoon marjoram
   ¼ teaspoon tarragon
   ¼ teaspoon rosemary
   2 tablespoons finely grated Parmesan cheese
   ¼ cup sesame seeds, lightly toasted*
   ½ teaspoon dry mustard (optional—for a sharper
      taste)

Please note:
   *To toast sesame seeds:

Place a skillet over medium heat. Add sesame seeds. Stir frequently for several minutes until seeds begin popping and turn *slightly* darker in color. Be careful—they burn quickly.

Lemon-Cucumber Dressing

Makes: 1 quart

Lemony-sweet dressing with a hint of dill.

Preparation time: 12-15 minutes

Blend in blender:
1 cup fresh lemon juice
½ cup oil (preferably olive or sesame)
3 large cucumbers, peeled and coarsely chopped
3 tablespoons honey
4¼ teaspoons tamari
¾ teaspoon dried dill or more, to taste
½ teaspoon garlic powder or more, to taste

While blending, add:
¾ cup sunflower seeds

Lemon-Parsley Salad Dressing

Makes: 3 cups

Preparation time: 15 minutes

Blend in blender:
1 cup vegetable oil
4 teaspoons apple cider vinegar
½ cup lemon juice
2 cups (packed) fresh parsley
½ teaspoon marjoram
⅓ cup chopped green bell pepper
1 teaspoon salt
dash black pepper

Lemon-Tahini Dressing

Makes: 2 cups

A light, airy tahini dressing.

Preparation time: 20 minutes

In a blender, combine:
½ cup olive oil
4 tablespoons lemon juice

Add and blend:
1 large clove garlic
3 tablespoons minced onion
2 stalks celery with leaves, chopped
2 tablespoons chopped fresh parsley
⅛ teaspoon salt

Add and blend:
½ cup sesame tahini

Tahini Dressing

Makes: 1½ cups

Good with salads. Wonderful on sesame-tofu burgers (page 119).

Preparation time: 10 minutes

Blend in blender:
- ½ cup water
- ½ cup tahini
- 2 tablespoons tamari (use ¼ cup for dressing for burgers)
- ¼ cup apple cider vinegar
- ½ teaspoon garlic powder
- ½ teaspoon dried dill weed
- ¼ cup barley malt syrup
- ¼ cup sesame seeds
- ½ teaspoon mixed herb seasoning (we recommend Vegit, which can be found in most health food stores)

Add water to thin if necessary. This dressing is thick and pungent. Those who like the flavor of tahini will enjoy it.

Tamari Salad Dressing

Makes: 2 cups

Surprisingly good!

Preparation time: 5-8 minutes

Blend in blender:
- 1 cup safflower oil
- ½ cup apple cider vinegar
- ¼ cup tamari
- ¼ cup honey

Variations:

Add any one or more of the following:

¼ cup nutritional yeast or more, to taste
herbal seasoning, to taste
1 teaspoon basil or, to taste

Poppy Seed Dressing

Makes: 2½-3 cups

Sweet and creamy.

Preparation time: 10 minutes

Blend in blender:
½ cup water
¼ to ½ cup honey or to taste
¼ cup apple cider vinegar
2 tablespoons prepared mustard
3 rounded tablespoons chopped onions
1 tablespoon poppy seeds
1 teaspoon salt

Slowly add and blend with rest of mixture:
1½ cups safflower or sesame oil

This dressing is especially good on spinach salad.

Tropical Blend
Fruit Salad Dressing

Makes: 2½-3 cups

Preparation time: 10-15 minutes

Combine in blender until smooth:
  1½ cups cream
  1 cup ripe mango pulp
  ½ tablespoon minced fresh mint
  2 tablespoons honey, to taste
  ¼ cup ground almonds

Orange-Cream
Fruit Salad Dressing

Makes: 3 cups

Preparation time: 10 minutes

Combine in blender until smooth:
1½ cups cream
½ cup freshly squeezed orange juice
½ avocado or 1 banana
2 tablespoons honey or, to taste
½ cup chopped dates, raisins, or currants

Avocado-Orange
Fruit Salad Dressing

Makes: 1-2 cups

Preparation time: 10 minutes

Combine in blender until smooth:
juice of 3-4 medium oranges (depending on how
    thick you like your dressing)
1 avocado
2 small bananas (or 1 large)
½ cup ground almonds

Vegetables, Side Dishes

Lemon-Herb Cauliflower

Serves: 8

Preparation time: 20-25 minutes
Baking time: 15-20 minutes

Preheat oven to 375°. Break into florets and steam until crisp-tender:

2 large heads cauliflower (about 5 pounds)

While the above cooks, sauté for several minutes:

1 cube butter (½ cup)
3 large cloves garlic, pressed

Add:

¾ teaspoon basil
¾ teaspoon oregano
salt and black pepper, to taste
5 tablespoons fresh lemon juice or more, to taste

Arrange cauliflower in a 2½-quart baking dish. Add butter mixture and stir well. Sprinkle with:

1 cup finely grated fresh Parmesan cheese
paprika

Bake at 375° for 15-20 minutes until golden brown and cheese is melted.

Italian Green Beans

Serves: 5-6

Preparation time: 25-30 minutes

Cook in boiling salted water until crisp-tender:
2 pounds frozen Italian green beans

While the above cooks, sauté until golden:
¼ cup olive oil
2 tablespoons butter
4 large cloves garlic, minced
1 medium-large onion, chopped

Drain beans and add to onions and garlic along with:
½ cup minced fresh parsley
3 tablespoons fresh lemon juice
1½ teaspoons marjoram
salt and black pepper, to taste

Cook until beans are heated through and serve.

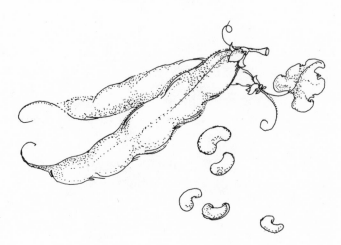

Pakoras

Serves: 6-8

Deep fried vegetable croquettes with Indian spices.

Preparation time: 50 minutes
Frying time: 30 minutes

Grate or mince:

4 cups fresh spinach (leaves only)
2 cups cauliflower

Add:

1 tablespoon cumin powder
1 tablespoon turmeric
1 tablespoon coriander
¾ teaspoon cayenne
⅜ teaspoon ground cloves
⅜ teaspoon cardamon
¾ teaspoon cinnamon
⅜ teaspoon curry powder
4 large cloves garlic, pressed
1 tablespoon finely grated fresh ginger
1 tablespoon salt
¼ cup lemon juice
½ cup chopped Ortega green chiles

Add and mix well, forming a medium-thick batter:

3 cups garbanzo flour or more, as needed
water, if needed

Drop batter by spoonfuls into:

**1 quart hot peanut oil (use processed commercial
    variety)**

Fry pakoras until dark golden brown. Remove with slotted spoon and drain on paper towels. Serve hot.

Herbed Carrots

Serves: 6

Foolproof and fabulous!
Preparation time: 45-50 minutes

Sauté until golden:

4 tablespoons butter
3 tablespoons olive oil
3 tablespoons minced onion
2 large cloves garlic, minced

Add and cook for 5 more minutes:

2 pounds carrots, sliced into thin rounds

Add, stir, cover, and cook for 10 more minutes:

2 teaspoons honey
2 bay leaves
1 cup dry white wine

Add:

4 tablespoons chopped fresh parsley
1 tablespoon basil
salt and black pepper, to taste
freshly grated nutmeg, to taste

Increase heat to medium-high and cook uncovered until
carrots are crisp-tender and liquid has evaporated.
Remove bay leaves and serve.

Potatoes Sautéed with Unpeeled Garlic

Serves: 4

A flavorful French dish appropriate for breakfast or dinner.

Preparation time: 15 minutes
Cooking time: 25-35 minutes

Lightly scrub and chop into $^1/_2$-1 inch dice:

$3^1/_2$ pounds boiling potatoes (Sounds like a lot, but watch them disappear!

Set them aside on paper towels.

Divide between two large skillets:

$^2/_3$ cup olive oil

Heat skillets over medium heat and add:

18 whole cloves *unpeeled* garlic (9 in each pan)

Fry the garlic over medium heat for 2 minutes. Pat the potatoes dry and add them to the pans in a single layer for more even browning. Sauté them until they are golden, stirring every few minutes. When golden (yet not necessarily tender), add a sprinkling of salt. Cover pans, reduce heat, and continue to cook until tender.

Add:

Salt to taste

Serve hot, garnished with:

$1^1/_2$ tablespoons minced chives
$1^1/_2$ tablespoons minced parsley

Note:

Traditionally, the garlic is discarded before serving, but we find slipping the skins off and eating the tender garlic to be a delicious treat with the potatoes.

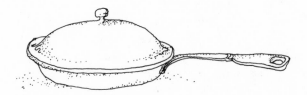

Cumin Sweet Potatoes

Serves: 5-6

A spicy, aromatic blend of Middle-Eastern flavors.

Preparation time: 25-30 minutes

Sauté in large skillet over medium heat for 15 minutes:
   4-6 tablespoons butter
   2 large onions, cut into chunks
   2 pounds sweet potatoes (slender if possible), peeled
      and cut into ¼-inch slices

Add and cook until cumin seed has browned and vegetables are tender:
   3 large green bell peppers, cut into chunks
   2½ tablespoons cumin seed (not powder)
   salt or tamari, to taste

Please note:
   You may steam sweet potatoes until crisp-tender instead of sautéeing them, but be careful not to overcook.

Sweet and Sour Vegetables   Serves: 6-8

Very colorful.

Preparation time: 45 minutes

In a large saucepan, bring to a boil and cook until thickened:

$^1/_8$ cup tomato purée
$^1/_4$ cup soy sauce
$^1/_3$ cup honey
$^1/_4$ cup cooking sherry
3 tablespoons cornstarch (dissolved in pineapple juice)
$^1/_4$ cup rice vinegar or cider vinegar
$^1/_2$ cup unsweetened pineapple juice

While the sauce is cooking, steam until crisp-tender:

2 cups sliced carrots
1 cup chopped onion
1 tablespoon fresh grated ginger root

Then turn off heat, add and cover:

2 cups chopped bok choy or other greens (The heat from the pan will cook bok choy.)

Add steamed carrots, onions and bok choy to the sauce. Then add:

2 cups chopped green peppers
2 cups chopped unsweetened pineapple
1 small can drained sliced water chestnuts
3 cups chopped tomatoes

Cook until thickened. Serve with rice or noodles.

Sautéed Spinach
Oriental Style

Serves: 4-6

Preparation time: 30-40 minutes

Sauté over high heat in large skillet, stirring often, until spinach is tender and liquid is almost evaporated:

3 tablespoons butter
½ teaspoon sesame oil or more, to taste
3 pounds fresh spinach, coarsely chopped (leaves only)
3 tablespoons tamari or more, to taste
½ tablespoon honey
2 tablespoons mirin (sweet cooking sake) or dry sherry

Remove spinach with slotted spoon and form a mound in the center of a large serving platter. Add to skillet and sauté about 3 minutes, stirring often, until crisp-tender:

2 tablespoons tamari or more, to taste
½ teaspoon sesame oil or more, to taste
12 ounces mung sprouts

Remove sprouts with slotted spoon and arrange in a circle around spinach. Sauté until warmed through in the remaining oil-tamari mixture:

one 8-ounce can water chestnuts, drained and sliced

Garnish spinach with water chestnuts. Sprinkle over top:

1 tablespoon toasted sesame seeds

Burnt Eggplant

Serves: 6

A traditional Indian side dish.
The burnt flavor is part of its uniqueness.

Preparation time: 50-55 minutes

How to "burn" an eggplant: Cook eggplant over an open flame by placing it directly on gas burner. Rotate eggplant to char all sides evenly. Eggplant will gradually collapse as flesh becomes soft.

Burn and set aside to cool:

5 medium-large eggplants

Sauté in large skillet or saucepan over medium-low heat until garlic and onions are transparent:

½ cup butter
2 large cloves garlic, pressed, or more, to taste
½ large onion, finely grated (including juice)
1½ teaspoons salt or more, to taste
¼ yellow chile, minced (use more for a hotter version)

Spoon cooled insides of eggplants into the sauce and mix well. Bring the mixture to a boil so that the sauce saturates the eggplant.

Scalloped Corn

Serves: 8

Preparation time: 15 minutes
Baking time: 45- 50 minutes

Preheat oven to 375°. Butter a deep 2¹/₂ quart baking
dish. Combine the following ingredients and pour
into dish:

3¼ cups fresh or frozen corn
5 eggs, beaten
2¾ cups half and half or cream
5 tablespoons butter, melted
3 tablespoons whole wheat pastry flour
¼ cup finely chopped onion
½ cup finely chopped green bell pepper
1½ teaspoons salt
¼ teaspoon black pepper
¼ teaspoon paprika

optional: a dab of honey to sweeten

Bake at 375° for 45-50 minutes, or until pudding is
golden brown and a knife inserted in the center comes
out clean.

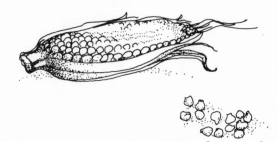

Herbed Millet

Serves: 3-4

Preparation time: 20 minutes
Cooking time: 30 minutes

Sauté in saucepan until onions are transparent:

4 tablespoons vegetable oil
½ large or 1 small onion, minced
2 cloves garlic, minced

Add:

½ teaspoon thyme
½ teaspoon basil
1½ teaspoons minced fresh parsley
½ teaspoon tarragon
½ teaspoon herb seasoning (Vegit or Spike)
⅛ teaspoon salt (eliminate if salted vegetable bouillon cube is used)
pinch of black pepper

Stir in:

1 cup raw millet

After stirring a few minutes, add:

2 cups boiling water
1 Huegli vegetable bouillon cube

Cover and simmer for 30 minutes.

Sesame Rice

Serves: 4-6

Preparation time: 25 minutes
Cooking time: 1 hour

Bring to a boil:

3 cups water

Add and once again bring to a boil:

1½ cups short grain brown rice

Reduce heat, cover, and simmer until liquid is
absorbed (35-45 minutes). While rice cooks, sauté until
golden brown, stirring frequently:

1 tablespoon butter
2 tablespoons chopped cashews

Remove and set aside. Heat:

3 tablespoons butter

Add and fry until seeds are golden brown, stirring
frequently:

½ cup sesame seeds
¼ teaspoon cayenne or more, to taste
1 bay leaf, crumbled

Combine cashews and sesame seeds and stir into hot
cooked rice. Add:

½ teaspoon salt or, to taste

Mix thoroughly. Sprinkle with:

juice of ½ lime
1 tablespoon rose water (optional)

Lemon Rice

Serves: 4

Preparation time: 15 minutes
Cooking time: 50-65 minutes

Bring to a boil:
3 cups water

Add and once again bring to a boil:
1¹/₂ cups basmati rice

Reduce heat to simmer and simmer until liquid is
absorbed (35–45 minutes). While rice cooks, lightly
sauté in large skillet over medium heat until golden
brown:
¹/₂ cup chopped onion
2 tablespoons butter

Add and cook until mustard seeds start to pop:
4 tablespoons butter (half a cube)
1 teaspoon black mustard seeds
pinch-¹/₈ teaspoon cayenne
2 teaspoons turmeric
1 bay leaf, crumbled
¹/₂ teaspoon salt (if cooked rice is unsalted)

Add cooked rice and mix well. Then add:
2 tablespoons freshly squeezed lemon juice
2 tablespoons raisins
¹/₂-³/₄ cups frozen petite peas
1 tablespoon minced chives
1 tablespoon minced parsley

Cook until rice is warmed throughout.

Wild Rice-Chestnut Stuffing   Serves: 10

Preparation time: 40 minutes
Cooking time: 1 hour

> Sauté in large saucepan until golden and soft:
>> **6 tablespoons butter**
>> **12 ounces shallots, coarsely chopped**
>
> Add:
>> **1½ cups vegetable stock (6 unsalted vegetable
>> bouillon cubes dissolved in 1½ cups boiling
>> water)**
>> **8 ounces wild rice**
>> **1¼ cups dry white wine**
>> **¾ cup minced fresh parsley**
>> **1 teaspoon salt**
>> **¾-1 teaspoon black pepper**
>> **2 teaspoons basil**
>> **1 teaspoon sage**
>> **¾ teaspoon thyme**

Bring to a boil, then reduce heat to lowest setting and
cook covered until liquid is almost absorbed—about 50
minutes. When rice is almost done, sauté in skillet over
high heat until soft and liquid has evaporated:

> **4 tablespoons butter**
> **1 pound mushrooms, sliced**
> **1 cup chopped celery**

Add mushroom mixture to cooked rice, then stir in and
cook for an additional 5-10 minutes or until all liquid is
absorbed:

> **two 15½-ounce cans chestnuts, rinsed, drained and
> chopped**

Please note:

> If fresh chestnuts are available, use 1-1¼ pounds,
> blanched, peeled and coarsely chopped.

Breaded Mushrooms

Serves: 4

Preparation time: 40 minutes

Combine:
>½ cup whole wheat pastry flour
>½ teaspoon salt
>¼ teaspoon black pepper

Combine in a separate bowl:
>3 large egg yolks, beaten
>1 tablespoon water
>½ teaspoon salt
>½ teaspoon garlic powder
>¼ teaspoon black pepper
>pinch of cayenne

Crumble:
>3 slices toasted whole wheat bread

Wash, pat dry, and trim stalks of:
>½ pound large mushrooms

Coat mushrooms with flour mixture. Then dip coated mushrooms into egg yolk mixture. Roll mushrooms in bread crumbs, completely covering them. Melt in skillet:
>¼ cup butter
>¼ cup vegetable oil

Fry mushrooms over medium heat until golden brown on each side and tender when pierced with a fork. Watch closely. They burn easily. After both sides are browned you can cover skillet with a lid to speed up cooking time.

Serving suggestions:
>Sprinkle with freshly grated Parmesan cheese or serve with a dip or sauce.

Main Dishes

Broccoli-Noodle
Casserole with Cheese

Serves: 3-4

Preparation time: 30 minutes
Baking time: 20 minutes

Preheat oven to 400°. Bring to a boil:

8 cups water

Add to boiling water and cook until almost tender:

2 cups elbow macaroni
1 teaspoon oil
dash of salt

Drain noodles, rinse with cold water, and place in large casserole dish. While macaroni cooks, sauté until golden in medium-large skillet:

2 tablespoons butter
1 medium onion, chopped
1 clove garlic, minced
1 teaspoon dried parsley
pinch black pepper
3 tablespoons tamari
½ teaspoon paprika

Add and sauté (covered) until tender:

1 zucchini, sliced
2 cups chopped broccoli
1 medium tomato, chopped

Spoon sautéed vegetables over macaroni. Add and mix well:

1½ cups grated cheddar cheese

Sprinkle over top:

¼-½ cup fresh whole wheat bread crumbs

Bake at 400° for 20 minutes.

Tostaditos

Yield: 4 tostaditos or 2-4 servings

Great for lunch or dinner.

Preparation time: 25 minutes
Bakes: 6-8 minutes

Preheat oven to 425°.

Prepare the following ingredients keeping them separated for individual use:

4 chopped mushrooms
2 chopped green onions
1 large or 2 medium diced tomatoes
$^3/_4$ of a green pepper, diced
1$^1/_2$ cups mung bean sprouts
$^3/_4$ cup black olives
4 cups grated cheddar

Then lay on a foil-covered baking sheet (for easy clean-up):

4 whole wheat chappatis

Sprinkle each chappati with the vegetables. Cover them with the cheese. Bake at 425° for 6-8 minutes until the cheese is thoroughly melted and edges of the chappatis are beginning to brown. Serve topped with:

sour cream
salsa

Swiss Cheese Fondue

Serves: 4

Preparation time: 35-40 minutes

Crush with the flat of a knife:
1 clove garlic

Remove the skin and rub the bottom and sides of the fondue pot with the garlic. Discard the garlic.

Add to the pot:
2 cups Reisling wine

Heat until bubbles rise. While wine heats, cube:
1 pound long loaf French bread (Every piece should have some crust to help it to hold together when dipped in the cheese.)

Add to the wine, stirring with a wooden fork:
10 ounces gruyère cheese, grated
10 ounces Emmenthal cheese, grated

Add:
1 tablespoon potato flour or potato starch
1 tablespoon kirsh
3 pinches freshly grated nutmeg
freshly ground white pepper, to taste

Continue cooking, stirring with the wooden fork until the cheese and wine blend.

Deep Dish
Russian Vegetable Pie

Serves: 4-5

Preparation time: 60 minutes
Baking time: 35 minutes

Preheat oven to 400°. To make pastry, double pie crust recipe (page 190). Roll out ⅔ of the pastry and line a remaining pastry onto waxed paper and make a circle large enough to cover the dish. Chill pastry circle.

Sauté in medium skillet over medium-high heat, stirring constantly:

2 tablespoons butter
1 small head cabbage, coarsely shredded
1 yellow onion, peeled and chopped

Add, stirring frequently:

⅛ teaspoon marjoram
⅛ teaspoon tarragon
⅛ teaspoon basil
salt, to taste
⅛ teaspoon freshly ground black pepper

Allow mixture to cook until cabbage is wilted and onions are soft. Remove from skillet and set aside. Sauté in the same pan for 5 or 6 minutes, stirring constantly:

2 tablespoons butter
½ pound mushrooms, sliced

On the bottom of the pie shell, spread:

4 ounces softened cream cheese

Top cheese with a layer of:

4-5 hard-boiled eggs, sliced

Sprinkle eggs with:

⅛ teaspoon dried dill weed

Cover with cabbage, mushroom mixture, and the circle of pastry. Press pastry together tightly at edges and flute them. With a sharp knife, cut a few short slashes through the top crust. Bake at 400° for 15 minutes, then turn the temperature down to 350° and continue baking for another 20-25 minutes or until the crust is light brown.

Italian Vegetable Casserole

Serves: 8

Preparation time: 35 minutes
Baking time: 1½ hours

Preheat oven to 375°. Finely chop and mix together:
  2 medium carrots
  2 stalks celery
  3 large cloves garlic

Add:
  ½ cup minced fresh parsley
  2 teaspoons oregano
  salt and black pepper, to taste

Oil a 4-quart casserole dish with olive oil and place in layers, alternating with the carrot and celery mixture:
  3 medium red onions, thinly sliced
  3 medium red or green bell peppers, cut into ¼-inch rings
  4 medium red potatoes, cut into ⅛-inch rounds
  4 medium zucchini, cut into ⅛-inch rounds

Drizzle each layer and the top of the casserole with:
  olive oil (approximately ⅓ cup)

Bake at 375° for 1½ hours until tender. If the top gets too brown, cover dish with foil. Stir well before serving, and pour off any excess oil.

Russian Beet Casserole

Serves: 4

Surprisingly good with a lovely pink color.

Preparation time: 20 minutes
Total cooking time: 30 minutes

Preheat oven to 400°.

Steam until soft:
   3½ cups peeled and chopped beets (about 6
      medium sized)
   1¾ chopped onion

Mix with:
   2½ cups grated sharp cheddar
   Scant 1 cup plain yogurt
   ⅛ teaspoon each salt and black pepper

Bake 10 minutes. The cheese seems to disappear if
overcooked.

Serve over rice, noodles or toast.

Scalloped Potatoes with Cheese and Broccoli

Preparation time: 40 minutes
Cooking time: 45-50 minutes

Preheat oven to 350°. Slice into $^1/_8$-inch to $^1/_4$-inch slices and steam until tender:

4-5 baking potatoes ($2^1/_2$ pounds)

Steam until tender:

$1^1/_2$ cups chopped broccoli (Peel the stalks before chopping.)

In a buttered 8-inch square pan, layer in the following order:

$^1/_3$ of the cooked potatoes
$1^1/_2$ tablespoons of butter dotted over the potatoes
$^1/_8$ teaspoon salt
$^1/_8$ teaspoon garlic powder
$1^1/_2$ tablespoons flour
$^1/_2$ cup grated medium cheddar cheese
1 tablespoon freshly grated Parmesan cheese
$^1/_2$ cup thinly sliced onions
freshly ground black pepper

Repeat the above, using steamed broccoli instead of onions. Top with the remaining potatoes.

Pour over mixture:

2 cups milk

Sprinkle top with:

1 tablespoon Parmesan, or to taste
paprika

Bake for 45-50 minutes at 350°.

Spicy Potato Casserole

A good company dish.

Preparation time: 40-45 minutes
Baking time: 15-20 minutes

Preheat oven to 400°. Cook in salted water until tender, then drain:

**8 medium-large potatoes (about 4½ pounds), cut into
small cubes**

While potatoes are cooking, grate:

2 cups (packed) cheddar cheese

Finely chop and set aside:

**3 green onions, including tops
¼ cup fresh parsley
1 medium ripe tomato, peeled and seeded
1 stalk celery**

When potatoes are done, drain and mash them with:

**6 tablespoons butter
1⅜ teaspoons garlic powder
1 teaspoon salt or, to taste
¼ teaspoon cayenne
¼ teaspoon black pepper
1 cup cream**

Add vegetables and 1 cup of the grated cheese to potatoes. Spoon mixture into buttered 9-inch by 12-inch casserole dish, or large oven-proof baking dish. Top with
the remaining cup of cheese. Bake at 400° for 15-20 minutes or until cheese is golden brown.

Zucchini Casserole

Serves: 8-10

An excellent company dish.

Preparation time: 45 minutes
Baking time: 30 minutes

Preheat oven to 350°. In an oiled 9-inch by 12-inch
baking dish layer the following:

First layer—steam until crisp-tender:

**7-8 cups zucchini (about 3 pounds), cut in ¼-inch
rounds**

Second layer—a mixture of:

1 pint cottage cheese
1 pint sour cream
1 cup freshly grated Parmesan cheese
¼ teaspoon onion powder
¾ teaspoon garlic powder
4 rounded tablespoons minced fresh parsley
1½ teaspoons dried dill weed
¾ teaspoon salt
½ teaspoon black pepper
1 egg, beaten

Third layer—sauté in medium skillet until transparent:

3 tablespoons olive oil
2 medium-large onions, chopped

Add and cook until nearly all the liquid is absorbed:

1 pound mushrooms, sliced
2 tablespoons tamari

Fourth layer—a mixture of:

1 cup whole wheat bread crumbs
4 tablespoons melted butter
1¼ teaspoons basil
1¼ teaspoons marjoram
¼ teaspoon garlic powder
3 rounded tablespoons minced fresh parsley

Bake at 350° for 30 minutes.

Variations:

1. Add to bread crumb mixture:

8 tablespoons freshly grated Parmesan cheese

2. For a thicker bread crumb topping, increase the amount of bread crumbs and adjust seasonings and butter.

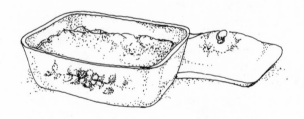

Stuffed Zucchini

Serves: 4

Preparation time: 45 minutes
Baking time: 30-40 minutes

Trim off ends and slice in half lengthwise:

8 small zucchini (about 5 inches long) or 4 large zucchini

Scoop out insides of zucchini and chop, leaving a shell
about ¼-inch thick. Set aside squash shells. In a large
skillet, sauté with chopped zucchini over medium heat
for a few minutes:

   1 tablespoon butter
   ¼ pound mushrooms, chopped
   1 tomato, chopped
   ½ large onion, finely chopped
   1 clove garlic, minced
   pinch thyme
   ⅛ teaspoon rosemary
   ¼ teaspoon basil

Increase heat to medium-high and cook, stirring
frequently for 10 minutes until the liquid is reduced to
⅓ of the original amount. Preheat oven to 350°.

While sautéeing, mix in a large bowl:

   2 eggs, beaten
   ¾ cup cottage cheese
   3 tablespoons fresh whole wheat bread crumbs (less
      than 1 slice)
   1 tablespoon tamari
   dash Worcestershire sauce
   ½ cup grated sharp cheddar cheese
   ¼ cup chopped walnuts

Place zucchini halves in buttered 11-inch by 13-inch
dish. Stuff zucchini generously. Sprinkle with:

   3 rounded tablespoons finely grated fresh Parmesan
      cheese

Bake at 350° for 30-40 minutes, depending on the size of
the zucchini.

Squash and Spinach Casserole   Serves: 6

Colorful and festive.

Preparation time: 55 minutes
Baking time: 25 minutes

Preheat oven to 375°. Combine in medium skillet and sauté until toasted (about 5 minutes):

3 tablespoons melted butter
2 cups (packed) fresh whole wheat bread crumbs
1 teaspoon garlic powder

Combine in a bowl:

1 cup cottage cheese
½ teaspoon basil
½ teaspoon thyme
¼ teaspoon powdered rosemary
½ teaspoon oregano

Add bread crumb mixture. Using the same skillet, lightly sauté until almost tender:

4 tablespoons butter
6 medium crookneck squash (cut into ⅛-inch rounds)

Place sautéed squash in shallow casserole dish. Sprinkle with:

salt and black pepper, to taste

Top with ½ of bread crumb mixture. Using the same skillet, cover and steam 1 to 2 minutes or until wilted:

2 tablespoons butter
2 bunches well-washed spinach (leaves only)

Top bread crumbs with drained spinach. Sprinkle with:

salt and black pepper, to taste

Bake uncovered at 375° for 15 minutes. Cover spinach

with remaining bread crumb mixture. Then top with:

3 medium tomatoes (cut into ½-inch slices)
1 cup (packed) shredded cheddar cheese

Bake for an additional 10 minutes or until cheese is melted.

Ratatouille

Serves: 4

A classic French dish delicious with steamed
new potatoes or a favorite bread.

Preparation time: 25-30 minutes
Cooking time: 50 minutes

Add to a large pot over medium heat until olive oil is warm:

¹/₂ cup olive oil

Add and sauté until onions are soft and transparent, stirring occasionally:

4 cloves garlic, minced
1¹/₂ cup chopped onion (about one large onion)

Stir in the following:

1 large eggplant (1^1/$_4$ pounds), cut in ^{1}/$_2$-inch
    cubes
1 green bell pepper
^{1}/$_2$ red bell pepper
2 large zucchinis (1 pound), cut in half lengthwise
    and chopped
^{1}/$_2$ pound mushrooms, quartered

Sauté, stirring frequently for a few minutes. Then add:

1 28-ounce can whole tomatoes with their juice
^{1}/$_2$ teaspoon basil
^{1}/$_4$ teaspoon oregano

Break the tomatoes up with a spoon. Simmer covered
for 25 minutes, stirring occasionally. Uncover and
continue cooking until vegetables are tender. Turn up
the heat and boil rapidly, stirring frequently until
most of the liquid has evaporated. Serve hot or at
room temperature.

Cabbage Casserole

Serves: 4-6

Preparation time: 50 minutes
Baking time: 50-60 minutes

Preheat oven to 350°. Spread in 2½-quart casserole dish:

**9 cups (packed) coarsely shredded cabbage (about
1½ large heads—we prefer the leafy, Napa
variety)**

Season with:

salt and black pepper

Cover cabbage with:

3 medium tomatoes, peeled, seeded, and chopped

Cook according to the package instructions until crisp,
then drain on a paper towel:

**one 5-ounce package stripples (available in health
food stores) or, to taste**

Crumble stripples over tomatoes. Sauté until wilted:

1 tablespoon butter
1½ large onions, coarsely chopped

Remove onions and place on top of stripples. In medium
skillet, melt:

2 tablespoons butter

Whisk in slowly:

3 tablespoons whole wheat pastry flour

When the flour has browned, gradually add, stirring
constantly but do not boil:

⅔ cup milk

Remove from heat and add:

⅔ **cup sour cream**
salt and black pepper, to taste

Spoon sauce over cabbage mixture. Sprinkle top with:

¾ **pound grated Muenster cheese**

Cover casserole dish with foil and bake at 350° for 20 minutes. Remove foil and continue baking for 30-40 minutes, or until cabbage is tender.

Rosanna's Risotto

Serves: 6-8

A risotto with champagne, cheeses and cream.
Serve with a nice salad and asparagus or artichokes on the side.

Preparation time: 35 minutes
Cooking time: 15-20 minutes

Bring to a boil then set aside:

5 cups water
1 unsalted vegetable bouillon cube
1 salted vegetable bouillon cube

In a large pot melt:

4 tablespoons butter (½ stick)

Add and stir frequently until golden:

⅓ **cup rounded minced purple onion**

Stir in and cook over medium heat for 2 minutes, stirring continuously:

2½ **cups Italian arborio rice (Uncle Ben's**
converted rice works well also.)

Add and stir for 1 minute until champagne becomes absorbed into the rice:

1 cup champagne

Add an additional:

¹/₄ cup champagne

Stir another 2 minutes. Add the broth. Bring to a boil, stirring occasionally. Reduce heat and simmer, *partially* covered with a lid, stirring occasionally for 15 to 20 minutes or until the liquid is absorbed. The rice will still look moist. Add:

¹/₂ cup cubed Jack cheese
³/₄ cup freshly grated Parmesan
2 tablespoons butter
¹/₂ cup heavy cream

Stir and cook over medium heat until cheeses are melted. Add:

1¹/₂ tablespoons minced parsley
¹/₈ teaspoon black pepper
salt, to taste
a large pinch *each* of dried basil, marjoram and
**   fines herbs (Use minced fresh herbs when**
**   available—about 1/4 teaspoon of each.)**

Stir in:

¹/₂ cup champagne

Serve with extra freshly grated Parmesan at the table.

In Milan, they sauté any leftover risotto in a thin layer until golden and crisp. It makes delicious rice cakes topped with freshly grated Parmesan.

Boboli Pizza

Serves: 3

Preparation time: 20 minutes
Cooking time: 8 minutes

Preheat oven to 450°. Make the **Quick Tomato Sauce** on page 147, or use ready-made sauce.

Have ready:

1 family size Boboli (1 pound Italian bread shell)

Get all ingredients ready to assemble. Spread on the Boboli:

1 cup tomato sauce
¼ large green bell pepper, thinly sliced and cut into pieces
2 large mushrooms, sliced

Mix together:

1 cup grated Jack cheese
1 cup grated Mozzarella
2 tablespoons freshly grated Parmesan

Cover the sauce and vegetables with the cheeses.

Top with:

¼ cup sliced black olives
6 marinated artichoke halves, sliced lengthwise into thinner strips (remove any tough outer leaves)
1 tablespoon pine nuts
2 cloves garlic, minced

Bake in the preheated oven for 8 minutes. Serve, cut in wedges along with a crisp green salad.

Manicotti

Serves: 4

A family favorite.

Preparation time: 30 minutes (does not include home-made tomato
　　　　　　　　　　　sauce preparation)
Baking time: 40 minutes

Preheat oven to 375°. Prepare 5 cups tomato
sauce or have enough ready-made sauce for the manicotti. Lasagna Sauce (p.143) makes 5 cups, or use
Quick Tomato Sauce recipe (p.147). To make the
filling, mix together in a medium bowl:

1 1/2 cup ricotta
1 egg, slightly beaten
1 tablespoon minced parsley
1/4 cup freshly grated Parmesan
1/4 cup plus 2 tablespoons grated Jack cheese
1/2 rounded teaspoon basil
1/2 rounded teaspoon oregano
1/2 teaspoon freshly grated nutmeg
1/2 teaspoon salt
1/8 teaspoon black pepper
1/4 rounded teaspoon garlic powder

Stuff with the filling:
1 box (8) uncooked manicotti shells

Place in the bottom of an 8-inch glass square pan:
3 1/2 cups tomato sauce

Place the filled manicotti on top. Cover them with:
1 1/2 cups tomato sauce

Sprinkle with:
2-3 tablespoons freshly grated Parmesan

Bake at 375° for 40 minutes.

Macaroni and Cheese with Vegetables

Serves: 4

Preparation time: 25-30 minutes
Baking time: 20-25 minutes

Preheat oven to 350°. Bring to a boil:
6 cups water

Add and stir occasionally until tender (about 15 minutes):
2 teaspoons salt
2 cups vegetable macaroni elbows

Sauté in the butter for several minutes until soft:
1 1/2 tablespoons butter
1 small white onion, chopped

Add and cook until broccoli is tender:
2 cups chopped broccoli (peel the stems and chop into small bite-sized pieces)
10 mushrooms, cut in half and then sliced

Drain the macaroni when done and mix with:
2 1/2 cups grated cheddar
1 cup half 'n half
the cooked vegetables
3-4 teaspoons tamari
1/2 teaspoon garlic powder
cayenne, to taste

Place in a buttered casserole dish and sprinkle the top with:
1/2 cup grated cheddar
2 tablespoons raw sunflower seeds

Bake for 20-25 minutes.

Vegetable Curry

Serves: 6-8

Preparation time: 25-30 minutes

Sauté in large skillet over medium-high heat until seeds pop:

¼ cup peanut oil
4 teaspoons black mustard seeds

Lower heat. Add and continue to cook until onions are wilted:

2 large onions, chopped
4 teaspoons cumin seed
4 teaspoons turmeric
2 teaspoons coriander
2 teaspoons salt
½ teaspoon cayenne

Stir in:

10 cups cooked mixed vegetables (a good combination is cauliflower, broccoli and peas. You may also use leftover vegetables.)
1 cup yogurt

Simmer until vegetables are warmed throughout.

Cauliflower Curry

Serves: 4

Preparation time: 35 minutes

Sauté in large skillet until onions are soft:
1/4-1/2 cup butter
1 large onion, diced

Add:
2 teaspoons black mustard seeds

When seeds begin to pop, add:
2 cloves garlic, minced
2 teaspoons fresh grated ginger
1 tablespoon cumin powder
1 tablespoon plus 1 teaspoon curry powder (for a
    slightly milder flavor, use only 1 tablespoon curry
    powder)
1/2 teaspoon salt

Add, cover, and simmer until cauliflower is done:
1 large cauliflower, chopped or separated into florets
1/2 cup water or more as needed
2 large tomatoes, cut up, or 1 medium can
    (approximately 15 1/2 ounces) tomatoes (without
    juice)

When nearly done, add:
1 1/2 teaspoons lemon juice
1 cup frozen petite peas

Serve with rice.

Potato Curry with Peas

Serves: 3-4

A simple, light curry. Traditionally served over rice.

Preparation time: 25 minutes

Boil for 10 minutes or until tender when pierced with a fork, then drain:

4 cups diced boiling potatoes (3-4 medium potatoes)

Cook, then drain:

1¼ cups petite peas

Set potatoes and peas aside. In a large skillet|over medium-low heat, melt:

6 tablespoons butter (¾ stick)

Mix in and cook for 1 minute:

2 tablespoons curry powder

Then add:

½ cup half and half
salt, to taste

Add peas and potatoes to the curry sauce. Heat thoroughly. Garnish with:

1-2 tablespoons chopped fresh parsley

Potato-Mushroom Curry

Serves: 6-8

Preparation time: 35-40 minutes

Sauté over low heat in large covered saucepan until
thoroughly cooked (20-25 minutes):

¼ cup peanut oil
3 large onions, chopped
1½ pounds mushrooms, chopped
one 7-ounce can chopped Ortega chiles
6 large cloves garlic, minced
4 teaspoons grated fresh ginger

While the above is cooking, steam until tender, then
drain and set aside:

6 medium potatoes, cubed

After mushrooms are cooked, add:

1½ teaspoons turmeric
1½ teaspoons cumin powder
1½ teaspoons black pepper
2 teaspoons salt

Add potatoes to the curry mixture and heat through. Stir
in and heat thoroughly:

½ cup sour cream

Curried Rice with Vegetables and Cheese

Serves: 4

Preparation time: 45 minutes   (Includes 40 minutes for cooking the brown rice)

Place in a medium size pan and bring to a boil:

1¼ cup short grain brown rice
2½ cups water

After it comes to a boil, cover and reduce heat. Simmer for 35-40 minutes or until the liquid is absorbed. Meanwhile, sauté in a large frying pan for 3 minutes:

2 tablespoons butter (Add more if needed.)
1 white or yellow onion, chopped
1 clove garlic, minced

Add and continue to cook until all vegetables are tender:

1 zucchini, sliced and quartered
10 mushrooms, halved and sliced
¾ teaspoon curry powder
½ teaspoon cumin

Stir in and cook for only a few moments to heat:

½ cup mung bean sprouts

Remove pan from heat. Combine and reheat, if necessary, the cooked rice and vegetables. Add and stir until cheese is melted:

1½ cups grated medium cheddar cheese
1½ teaspoon tamari
⅛ teaspoon cayenne, or to taste

Serve.

Mushroom Polenta

Serves: 6

An excellent company dish, well worth the preparation time.

Preparation time: 1 hour
Cooking time: 2 hours
Baking time: 1½ hours
(Polenta and sauce can be made ahead of time and assembled and baked when needed.)

Mix well:
>2½ cups cold water
>1½ cups polenta meal (very coarse corn meal, available at health food and specialty stores)

Add mixture by spoonfuls to:
>2½ cups boiling water

Add and stir thoroughly:
>1¾ teaspoons salt

Cook mixture in double boiler (uncovered) over medium-low heat without stirring for 1½ hours. Butter a *deep* 8-inch or 9-inch square oven-proof pan and spoon polenta into it. Smooth top of mixture and let cool until firm. When completely set, run a knife along edges and turn out onto a large cookie sheet. With a sharp knife or string, split polenta into 3 even layers. Set aside. Meanwhile, prepare sauce and cheese, as follows:

Sauté until golden and set aside:
   1 cube butter (½ cup)
   1½ large onions, chopped
   3 large cloves garlic, minced

Wash and drain several times:
   1½ ounces dried mushrooms

Soak mushrooms for 15 minutes in:
   1½ cups hot water (drain and save the water)

Strain the water through several layers of cheese cloth 2-3 times and add, stirring until dissolved:
   2 unsalted vegetable bouillon cubes

Set the broth aside. Chop the reconstituted dried mushrooms, discarding tough stems, and add them to:
   2 cups (packed) coarsely chopped fresh mushrooms
   2 rounded tablespoons finely minced fresh parsley
   1½ teaspoons thyme
   1½ teaspoons basil
   scant ¼ teaspoon nutmeg

Add mixture to the sautéed onions and cook for 10 minutes or until mushrooms are tender. Add the mushroom broth and continue to cook over medium-high heat until liquid is reduced by ¾ (about 30 minutes).

Then add:

½ cup cream
salt and black pepper, to taste

While the mixture is cooking, thinly slice:

¾ pound Jack cheese

Prepare:

2 cups grated fresh Parmesan cheese
½ cup toasted whole wheat bread crumbs

Preheat oven to 350°. Butter the baking dish again and spread the bread crumbs on the bottom. Lay 1 slice of polenta on top of bread crumbs. Cover with ⅓ of the sliced Jack cheese, then ⅓ of the mushroom sauce, and top with ⅓ of the grated Parmesan cheese. Repeat the layers until all the ingredients are used, ending with the grated Parmesan cheese. Bake covered at 350° for 1 hour, then uncover and continue baking for ½ hour longer. (Dish will be very full.)

Please note:

If polenta layers fall apart in handling, gently piece them together. When you serve it, it *won't* fall apart.

Zucchini Patties

Serves: 4-6

A light vegetable burger.

Preparation time: 45 minutes

Steam until tender:
2 cups (packed) coarsely grated zucchini

Sauté in medium skillet until soft:
2 tablespoons oil
3 green onions, chopped (including tops)

Add to sautéed onions:
2 tablespoons (packed) minced fresh parsley
1 teaspoon basil

Combine in separate bowl:
1 cup (packed) fresh whole wheat bread crumbs
¼ cup (packed) toasted sunflower meal*
¼ cup cooked bulgur wheat or rice
½ teaspoon salt

Stir in:
2 beaten egg yolks

Combine all of the above ingredients. Beat until stiff, then fold into zucchini mixture:
whites of 2 eggs

Drop batter by spoonfuls onto lightly greased skillet and spread to form patties. Brown on both sides over medium heat. Serve with noodles or pilaf.

Please note:
*Toast sunflower seeds in dry frying pan over medium heat, stirring constantly until browned, then grind in blender until the consistency of fine meal.

Shish Kabob

Serves: 5-6

Try this on your barbeque with fresh corn on the cob.

Marinating time: 3 hours
Preparation time: 50 minutes
Cooking time: 5-10 minutes

Make marinade on page 233. Wash, trim off the stems and place in marinade for **several hours**:
   24 large mushrooms

Preheat oven to 400°. Cut into 1-inch cubes:
   18-24 ounces tofu

Spread the tofu in bottom of a well-buttered baking dish and bake 35-40 minutes, stirring every ten minutes. Pour most of the marinade from the mushrooms over the tofu and **marinate 1 hour.**

Blend briefly:
   1 16-ounce can whole tomatoes

Add and simmer for 30-60 minutes:
   the marinade
   1 tablespoon clover honey

Steam for 5 minutes:
   ¹/₂ each green and red bell pepper, cut into 1-inch pieces
   ¹/₄ white onion, cut into 1-inch pieces

Have ready along with the steamed vegetables:
   24 cherry tomatoes
   35 snow peas

Alternate vegetables and tofu on skewers, starting and ending with tofu to keep them secure. Baste with the tomato marinade sauce. Broil or barbeque for about 5-10 minutes, turning and basting often.   Serve with rice.

Sunburgers

Makes: 7 patties

Preparation time: 30 minutes (less if you use a food processor)
Baking time: 35 minutes

Preheat oven to 375°. Mix together:

    1½ cups ground sunflower seeds
    ½ cup grated carrots
    ½ cup finely chopped celery
    6 tablespoons minced onions
    2 tablespoons minced fresh parsley
    2 eggs
    1 teaspoon basil
    2 tablespoons tamari
    2 tablespoons melted butter
    1 teaspoon garlic powder

Drop mixture by large spoonfuls, forming patties, onto an oiled baking sheet. Bake at 375° for 20 minutes on one side and 10-15 minutes on the other side. Both sides should be a medium brown color. Serve on buns with mayonnaise, catsup, or your favorite condiments.

Sunny Sesame-Tofu Burgers

Serves: 6

A make-ahead low calorie meal.

Preparation time: 20 minutes
Baking time: 40 minutes

Preheat oven to 375°. Mix together in a large bowl:

**6 cakes tofu (1½ pounds) rinsed, squeezed, and
  kneaded**
⅓ cup sunflower seeds
¼ cup brown sesame seeds
1 stalk celery, minced
¼ cup minced onion

Add and knead together:

2 tablespoons tamari
**2 tablespoons Dr. Bronner's Liquid Bouillon (or
  1 vegetable bouillon cube dissolved in 2 tablespoons hot water)**
1½ teaspoons Spike (available at health food stores)
1 teaspoon garlic powder
**2 tablespoons dried or 6 tablespoons minced fresh
  parsley**

Add and gently mix:

3 cups alfalfa sprouts

Pack mixture firmly and evenly into a buttered baking
dish, approximately 6-inch by 10-inch. Sprinkle with
additional sesame seeds and pat down. Bake at 375° for
40 minutes. Cut into 3-inch by 3-inch "burgers", cool,
and store in the refrigerator.

To serve, spread Tahini Dressing (page 64) evenly on top
and reheat the burger for 10-20 minutes at 350°. Serve as
you would a burger.

Tofu-Spinach Combo

Serves: 4

Preparation time: 25-30 minutes

Sauté in large skillet over medium heat for 5 minutes:

2 tablespoons butter
1 large onion, chopped

Add and sauté for 8-10 minutes or until slightly brown:

2 cups bite-size tofu pieces

Add:

2 tablespoons tamari
1 teaspoon Vegit (available at health food stores)
pinch of cayenne

Add and stir until wilted (about 5-8 minutes):

1 pound fresh spinach, washed and chopped (leaves only)

Sprinkle with juice of:

1 large lemon

Serve over steamed brown rice.

Tofu Stroganoff

Serves: 4

Preparation time: 35 minutes

Rinse, then drain on paper towels to remove excess water:

1½ blocks *firm* tofu (18 ounces)

In a large skillet, sauté until onions are soft and transparent:

2 tablespoons butter
1 medium onion, chopped
10 mushrooms, thickly sliced
2 tablespoons dried chives
½-1 teaspoon garlic powder
¼ teaspoon salt
¼ teaspoon black pepper

Remove mixture from skillet and set aside. Add to skillet:

1 tablespoon butter plus 1 tablespoon vegetable oil

Brown tofu, sliced in strips, in 2 batches, using more butter and oil as needed. Add mushroom mixture to tofu. Just before serving, add:

2 cups sour cream
2-4 tablespoons tamari
1-2 tablespoons cooking sherry

Cook over low heat. Do not boil. To thin sauce, add more sour cream. Adjust sherry, to taste. Serve over noodles.

Scrambled Tofu

Serves: 2-3

Very much like scrambled eggs.

Preparation time: 15 minutes

> Mash with a fork:
> **2 packages tofu (18 ounces)**

> Melt in medium skillet over medium-low heat:
> **3 tablespoons butter**

> Sauté tofu in butter, then add:
> **1½-2 tablespoons tamari**
> **¼ teaspoon turmeric**
> **1 teaspoon onion powder**

Variations:

> Add one or more of the following:
> **curry powder**
> **herbs**
> **sautéed chopped vegetables**

Smothered Tofu

Serves: 4-5

Delicious on rice or mashed potatoes.

Preparation time: 50 minutes

> Sauté in large skillet over medium heat for 5 minutes, stirring occasionally:
> **½ cube butter (4 tablespoons)**
> **1½ cups chopped onions**

Add and continue to sauté until tender, stirring occasionally:

½ pound mushrooms, sliced

Remove mixture from pan and set aside. Mix together in a bag for shaking:

½ cup nutritional yeast (flaked variety)
½ cup whole wheat pastry flour

Mix in a bowl:

¼ cup tamari plus enough water to make ⅓ cup
1 teaspoon garlic powder
½ teaspoon basil
¼ teaspoon marjoram
¼ teaspoon thyme
pinch of cayenne

Cut into bite-size pieces:

2-2¼ pounds firm tofu

Melt in large skillet over medium heat:

½ cube butter

While melting butter, dip tofu quickly into tamari mixture, then place it in the bag with flour-yeast mixture and shake. Brown tofu in melted butter, stirring occasionally. (Tofu tends to crumble while cooking.) Mix together:

2 cups boiling water
1 unsalted vegetable bouillon cube

Add broth to browned tofu. Stir in onions and mushrooms. Let simmer for 5-10 minutes.

Baked Tofu with Cheese

Serves: 4-6

Preparation time: 15 minutes
Baking time: 20-25 minutes

Preheat oven to 350°. Slice into pieces ½-inch thick and arrange in a single layer in an oiled 9-inch by 12-inch baking dish:

1½ pounds tofu

Poke holes in tofu with fork and sprinkle with:

6 tablespoons tamari sauce
½ teaspoon garlic powder

Cover with:

6 ounces cheddar cheese, grated

Bake at 350° until a crust forms on the melted cheese—about 20-25 minutes, depending on how crunchy you like it.

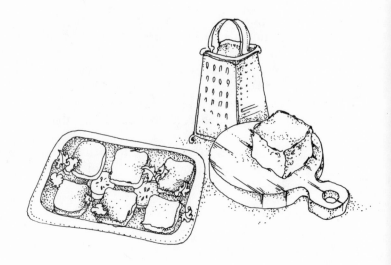

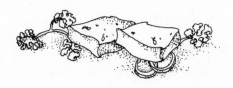

Tofu "Steaks"   Serves: 6

Preparation time: 23 minutes
Frying time: 35 minutes

To make marinade, mix together:
   ⅓ cup tamari
   ¼ cup cooking sherry
   2½ tablespoons grated fresh ginger
   2½ teaspoons garlic powder
   ½ cup water

Slice in pieces ¼-inch thick and marinate for
15 minutes, turning once:
   1½-2 pounds tofu

Brown tofu in 2 batches in large skillet over medium
heat, using:
   butter and oil

Keep first batch in a warm oven while second batch
cooks.

Nutty Cheese Cutlets
with Gravy

Serves: 6-8

One of our favorites! Great for non-vegetarians.

Preparation time: 50 minutes
Baking time: 30-35 minutes

Preheat oven to 375°. Soften and mash:

one 8-ounce package cream cheese

Stir in:

1½ cups chopped onion
¼ pound grated cheddar cheese (about ¾ cup)
3 eggs, beaten
1 cup chopped walnuts
1 cup cracker crumbs (about 4 large crackers. Ak-
Mak, available at health food stores, work well)
1 teaspoon oregano

Press mixture into small patties and brown over medium-high heat for 1-2 minutes on each side in:

vegetable oil

Place patties single layer in baking dish. Mix together:

2 cans undiluted cream of mushroom soup (We
use Campbell's.)
½ cup sour cream
1½ cups water
½ teaspoon garlic powder
¼ teaspoon oregano
¼ teaspoon beau monde
¼ teaspoon marjoram
¼ teaspoon thyme
¼ teaspoon sage

Pour ¾ of the sauce over the patties, covering each one, and bake at 375° for 20 minutes. Add the remainder of the sauce and bake for another 10-15 minutes. Delicious served with mashed potatoes or noodles.

Walnut Cheddar Loaf

Serves: 6-8

Delicious cold for sandwiches.

Preparation time: 40 minutes
Baking time: 1 hour

Preheat oven to 350°. Combine the following ingredients in a large bowl and set aside:

3 cups (packed) fresh whole wheat bread crumbs
1 cup (packed) ground walnuts
1 cup finely chopped walnuts
½ cup nutritional yeast
2 tablespoons tamari
½ cup tomato juice

Sauté in large skillet over medium heat until translucent:

4 tablespoons butter
2½ large onions, finely chopped
3-4 large cloves garlic, minced

Combine all of the above with:

2 well-beaten eggs
1 cup (packed) grated cheddar cheese
¼-½ teaspoon salt
½ teaspoon black pepper
2 tablespoons dried parsley *or* ¾ cup minced fresh parsley

Press into well-oiled loaf pan and bake at 350° for approximately 1 hour. Cover top of loaf with:

½ cup grated cheddar cheese

Bake for an additional 10 minutes or until cheese is bubbly. Serve as is, or with a gravy.

Spinach-Rice Casserole

Serves: 4 or 5

Excellent for light dinners or brunch.

Preparation time: 25 minutes
Baking time: 20-25 minutes

Cook for 40 minutes (see rice cooking instructions, page 82):

2 cups brown rice
4 cups water
1 salted vegetable bouillon cube

Cook according to package directions:

1 10-ounce package frozen spinach

Over medium-low heat melt the butter then add onion and garlic. Sauté until onion begins to soften:

1 tablespoon of butter
$^1/_4$ cup sliced green onion
2 cloves garlic, minced

Place the spinach in a medium-size bowl. Add:

$^3/_4$ cup grated Swiss or cheddar cheese
2 tablespoons minced fresh parsley
$^1/_2$ cup cottage cheese
$^1/_4$ cup sour cream
1 egg
1 teaspoon tamari
2 pinches freshly grated nutmeg

Preheat oven to 375°. Mix together the cooked rice and spinach mixture. Spoon into a buttered casserole dish. Top with:

6 tablespoons grated Swiss or cheddar cheese
(Whichever you used in with the spinach)
a sprinkling of cayenne or paprika

Bake at 375° for 20-25 minutes.

Egg Puff

Serves: 6-8

A mild egg, chile, and cheese dish.

Preparation time: 10-15 minutes
Baking time: 35 minutes

Preheat oven to 350°. Beat:

10 large eggs

Add and mix well:

½ cup whole wheat pastry flour
½ teaspoon baking powder

Mix in:

1 pint small curd cottage cheese
1 pound Jack or mild cheddar cheese, grated
¼ teaspoon salt
one 7-ounce can chopped Ortega green chiles

Spoon into 9-inch by 13-inch pan and bake at 350° for 35 minutes or until eggs are set. Serve with salsa.

Easy Cheese Soufflé

Serves: 4-5

Preparation time: 30-35 minutes
Baking time: 25-30 minutes

Preheat oven to 375°. Melt in medium saucepan over low heat:

6 tablespoons butter

Stir in:

6 tablespoons whole wheat pastry flour
¾ teaspoon salt
½ teaspoon black pepper
⅛ teaspoon cayenne

Slowly add and cook, whisking constantly until thick and smooth:

2 cups milk

Add and mix thoroughly:

1 cup (packed) grated sharp cheddar cheese

Remove mixture from heat and add gradually, whisking the entire time:

6 egg yolks, beaten

Gently fold in:

6 egg whites, stiffly beaten

Spoon into a buttered straight-sided or soufflé dish and bake at 375° for 25-30 minutes. Serve immediately or soufflé will fall. (Avoid drafts!) Excellent with Yogurt-Cheese Sauce (page 151) or Tomato-Sour Cream Sauce (page 146).

Variation:

Before adding soufflé mixture, layer in baking dish:

steamed or sautéed asparagus or broccoli

Penne with Fresh Tomatoes and Basil

Serves: 3-4

*Ripe garden-fresh tomatoes make all the difference
in this light, summery pasta dish.*

Preparation time: 45 minutes

Place a large kettle of water on the stove for the pasta
and bring to a boil. While waiting for the water to
come to a boil, get the following ingredients ready:

6 large, ripe tomatoes, peeled, seeded, and chopped
$^1/_2$ cup, rounded, chopped green onions
$1^3/_4$ cups chopped fresh basil
2 cloves garlic, minced
1 cup freshly grated Parmesan

Add to the large kettle of boiling water:

salt ($^1/_2$ tablespoon per quart of water)
**$2^1/_4$ cups penne or penne rigate shaped pasta (a
little more than half a pound)**

Cook the pasta, stirring occasionally until it is tender—about 12 minutes. While the pasta is cooking,
heat in a large frying pan over medium heat:

3 tablespoons olive oil

Add the chopped green onions and minced garlic and
stir until the onions are soft, 3-5 minutes. Add the
chopped tomatoes and cook another 3 minutes. Stir
in the chopped basil. Cook just until basil goes
limp—only a minute or so. When the pasta is done,
drain it well and place in a serving bowl, tossing it
with:

2 tablespoons butter

Add half the Parmesan cheese. Stir. Add the tomato-
basil sauce. Serve the remaining Parmesan at the
table for those who wish it.

Buon Appetito!

Savory Broccoli Quiche

Serves: 4-6

Yeast adds a rich full-bodied flavor.

Preparation time: 50 minutes (including making crust)
Baking time: 45 minutes

Preheat oven to 400°. Prepare a basic single pastry crust (page 190). Line a deep pie pan or a deep quiche pan with pastry and prick with a fork. Bake at 400° for 8-10 minutes. To make filling, steam until tender, then drain:

1 medium bunch of broccoli, chopped (about 2 cups)

Meanwhile, sauté in medium skillet over medium heat until golden:

2-4 tablespoons butter
1 medium-large onion, chopped

Add and blend well:

3 tablespoons nutritional yeast

Cook mixture over low heat for several minutes, remove from heat, and cool slightly. While onion mixture is cooling, prepare:

1½ cups (packed) grated Gruyère cheese

Place onion-yeast mixture on bottom of pre-baked pie shell. Sprinkle with ¾ of the grated cheese. Top with steamed broccoli. Combine:

4 eggs, beaten
1½ cups milk
¼ teaspoon salt
scant ½ teaspoon black pepper
⅛ rounded teaspoon nutmeg
scant ¼ teaspoon cayenne

Pour egg mixture over broccoli. Bake at 450° for 15 minutes, then turn heat down to 350° and add the rest of the grated cheese. Continue baking for 30 more minutes or until a knife inserted in center comes out clean.

Mushroom-Spinach Quiche

Serves: 6

Preparation time: 40 minutes
Baking time: 50 minutes
(See page 190 for pie crust)

Preheat oven to 375°. To make filling, sauté in large skillet over medium heat for 5 minutes or until mushrooms are soft:

4 tablespoons butter
5 green onions, chopped (including tops)
¾ pound mushrooms, sliced
1½ teaspoons garlic powder

Add to mushroom mixture and cook until liquid is almost evaporated:

10 ounces fresh spinach or one 10-ounce package frozen spinach, thawed and drained

Meanwhile, mix together:

4 eggs, beaten
1½ cups grated Swiss cheese
1¾ cups heavy cream or 1¾ cups half and half
¼ teaspoon nutmeg or, to taste
¼ teaspoon cayenne or, to taste
½ teaspoon salt or, to taste
½ teaspoon black pepper or, to taste

Combine all ingredients and pour into pre-baked pie shell. Sprinkle over top:

1½-3 tablespoons freshly grated Parmesan cheese
paprika

Bake at 375° for 40-50 minutes or until knife inserted in center comes out clean.

Gorgonzola Cream Sauce on Pasta Shells

Serves: 4

A sophisticated dish, very rich.

Preparation time: 20-25 minutes

Place a large pot of water on high heat for the pasta. While preparing the sauce, add to the water after it comes to a boil:

salt ($^1/_2$ tablespoon per quart of water)
$^3/_4$ pound pasta shells*

Meanwhile, in a medium small pot, bring to a boil:

2 cups (1 pint) whipping cream

Add and stir until blended:

$^1/_2$ cup cream cheese

Add and blend again:

$^1/_4$ to $^1/_2$ cup (4 to 8 ounces) *Italian* gorgonzola

Add:

$^1/_2$ cup freshly grated Parmesan
$^1/_8$ teaspoon freshly grated nutmeg
$^1/_4$ teaspoon freshly ground white pepper

Keep warm over low heat, or reheat later.

When the pasta is cooked just until tender, drain it and place in a serving bowl. Pour the sauce over the pasta and mix well. Garnish with:

freshly grated Parmesan

*$^1/_2$ pound tortellini may be substituted for the pasta shells.

Linguini with Pesto

Serves: 4-6

This pesto is great!

Preparation time: 20 minutes

Bring a large kettle of water to a boil. Meanwhile, combine in food processor or blender until fairly smooth:

2 cups fresh basil leaves
$^1/_2$ cup olive oil
2 tablespoons pine nuts
2 cloves of garlic, lightly crushed
$^1/_2$ teaspoon salt

Add to kettle of water, stirring occasionally:

1 pound dried linguini
salt ($^1/_2$ tablespoon per quart of water)

While pasta cooks, complete the pesto by stirring together in a small bowl the basil mixture with:

$^1/_2$ cup plus 2 tablespoons freshly grated
Parmesan ($2^1/_2$ ounces)
3 tablespoons softened butter

Drain linguini when tender. Mix with the pesto. Garnish with extra Parmesan at the table for those who wish it.

To freeze pesto: withhold the cheese and butter. Add when thawed.

Hungarian Noodles

Preparation time: 15-20 minutes
Baking time: 30 minutes

Preheat oven to 350°. Cook in salted water until almost tender:

½ pound fettucine noodles (sesame or soy-corn)

Drain and combine with:

1 cup cottage cheese
1 cup sour cream
¼ cup (packed) finely chopped green onions
2 large cloves garlic, minced
1 tablespoon poppy seeds
1 tablespoon tamari

Bake in an 8-inch square baking dish at 350° for 30 minutes. Sprinkle top with:

½ cup (packed) freshly grated Parmesan cheese
¼ teaspoon paprika

Bake for 5 minutes more or until cheese melts.

Mushroom Spaghetti

Serves: 5-6

Preparation time: 25 minutes

Cook until almost tender in salted water:

1 pound sesame spaghetti

While preparing spaghetti, sauté in medium skillet over medium heat and set aside:

3 tablespoons olive oil
1 pound mushrooms, sliced
¾ teaspoon salt
1 teaspoon black pepper

In a serving bowl, mix hot spaghetti with:

1 egg, beaten
7 tablespoons freshly grated Parmesan cheese
2 tablespoons butter
1 tablespoon olive oil

Top with sautéed mushrooms.

Variation:

Add one or both of the following:

onion sautéed in olive oil
cheese and an extra egg

Lasagna

Serves: 6-8

Preparation time: 1½ hours
Cooking time (sauce): 1 hour
Baking time: 45 minutes-1 hour

To make filling, sauté in large skillet over medium heat
for 5 minutes:

⅓ cup olive oil
1½ cups chopped onions
4 cloves garlic, minced

Add and sauté 5 minutes more:

1½ cups sliced zucchini, cut into ¼-inch rounds

Add and cook another 5 minutes or until mushrooms and
zucchini are tender:

6 cups sliced mushrooms (about 1 pound)
½ teaspoon basil
¼ teaspoon salt
⅛-¼ teaspoon black pepper
⅛ teaspoon cayenne

To cook noodles, cook in a large saucepan for 15 minutes
or until almost tender:

1 pound lasagna noodles (we prefer sesame)
1 tablespoon vegetable oil

Rinse under cold water and set aside.

Prepare cheeses:

4 ounces thinly sliced Jack cheese
10 ounces thinly sliced mozzarella cheese
¼-½ cup (packed) grated fresh Parmesan cheese
1⅓ cups ricotta cheese (a little less than 1 pound)

Preheat oven to 350°. To assemble, oil a *deep* 9-inch by
11-inch pan. Layer in pan in the following order:

1 cup tomato sauce (see below)
⅓ of the noodles
⅔ cup ricotta cheese
½ of the mushroom mixture
the Jack cheese
1 cup tomato sauce
1 tablespoon Parmesan cheese or more, to taste
half the remaining noodles
⅔ cup ricotta cheese
rest of mushroom mixture
4 ounces mozzarella cheese (less than half)
last of the noodles
1¾ cups tomato sauce
rest of mozzarella cheese

Top with:

remaining Parmesan cheese
⅓ cup sliced black olives

Bake at 350° for 45 minutes-1 hour.

To make tomato sauce (5 cups), sauté in large
saucepan over medium heat for 5 minutes:

½ cup olive oil
2 cups finely chopped onions
3 cloves garlic, minced

Add and simmer for 1 hour:

2 large (28-ounce) cans tomatoes
6 ounces tomato paste
2 tablespoons minced fresh parsley
1 teaspoon salt
1½ tablespoons honey
1 rounded teaspoon oregano
1 rounded teaspoon basil
¼ teaspoon black pepper
1 cup water
⅛ teaspoon cayenne or, to taste

Sauces, Dips & Spreads

Tomato-Sour Cream Sauce
Makes: 7 cups

An unusual, versatile sauce.

Preparation time: 20-25 minutes
Cooking time: 30-35 minutes

Blanch (to remove skins) by dropping into boiling water:

6 large tomatoes

After several minutes remove with slotted spoon and immediately plunge into cold water. Slip the skins (they come right off). Slice tomatoes and place in heavy saucepan. Add:

4 tablespoons butter
3 large onions, sliced into thin rounds, then cut in half

Cook over low heat for 30-35 minutes, stirring occasionally. When sauce is almost done, add the following seasonings to taste:

salt
black pepper
garlic powder
basil

After sauce has cooked, remove from heat and stir in:

1 pint sour cream

Use as an omelet filling or as a sauce for fritata or pasta.

Quick Tomato Sauce

Makes: 3 cups

Preparation time: 15 minutes
Cooking time: 20-30 minutes

In a medium-sized saucepan lightly heat:
3 tablespoons olive oil

Add and simmer stirring frequently for three minutes, or until onions become translucent:
2 cloves garlic, minced
1 cup chopped yellow onion

Stir in:
2 15-ounce cans tomato sauce
$^3/_4$ teaspoon basil
$^3/_4$ teaspoon oregano
salt and pepper to taste
pinch of sugar

Simmer sauce over medium-low heat, stirring occasionally, for 20-30 minutes.

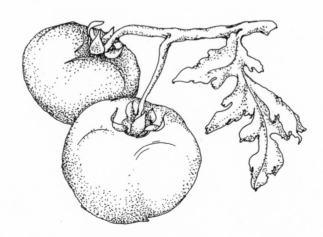

Spaghetti Sauce
with Mushrooms
Makes: 10-12 cups

A wonderful all-purpose sauce.

Preparation time: 50 minutes
Cooking time: 45 minutes-1 hour

Sauté in large saucepan over medium heat until onions
are transparent:

½ cup olive oil
4 medium onions, chopped
7 large cloves garlic, minced
4 large green bell peppers, chopped
¾ pound mushrooms, thickly sliced

Add and simmer for about an hour:

6 small bay leaves (remove after 30-35 minutes of
    cooking)
1 teaspoon garlic powder
4 pounds canned tomatoes with juice, coarsely chop-
    ped (if using fresh tomatoes, add a little tomato
    juice)
12 ounces tomato paste
    honey to taste
1½ teaspoons salt
1 teaspoon ground dried thyme
1 teaspoon ground dried oregano
1 tablespoon basil
1 teaspoon black pepper
1 teaspoon chile powder
½ teaspoon cumin powder
½ cup minced fresh parsley

Variations:

1. Add sautéed or steamed vegetables to sauce (eggplant,
peas, zucchini, cauliflower). Add vegetables during last
20 minutes of cooking.

2. Add to pasta and mix well just before serving:
ricotta cheese, to taste

Pesto-Ricotta Spread

Makes: 2¹/₄-2¹/₂ cups

Superb.

Preparation time: 20-25 minutes

Blend in food processor or blender until fairly smooth:
2 cups fresh basil leaves
¹/₂ cup olive oil
2 tablespoons pine nuts
2 cloves garlic, lightly crushed
¹/₂ teaspoon salt

Pour mixture into a bowl and stir in well:
¹/₂ cup plus 2 tablespoons freshly grated
  Parmesan (2¹/₂ ounces)
3 tablespoons softened butter

Add:
1¹/₄ cups ricotta cheese

Try one of the following variations, or create your
own:
1. Use as a spread for sandwiches.
2. Try open-faced on French bread with sliced
   tomatoes at a picnic.
3. Mix 2 eggs with the filling and use in manicotti
   (page 106) instead of the regular filling. Bake as
   directed with the tomato sauce.
4. Use in omelettes.
5. Swirl onto pizza.

To freeze: withhold the cheese and butter. Add when
thawed.

Tofu-Yogurt Sauce

Makes: 2¾ cups

An excellent, low-calorie sauce. Use as a vegetable dip or as a filling for enchiladas, manicotti, or lasagna.

Preparation time: 10 minutes

> Blend until smooth (for tofu, a food processor works better than a blender):
>
> **1 pound tofu**
> **2 tablespoons tahini**
> **2 tablespoons red miso**
> **4 teaspoons tamari**
> **1 cup yogurt**
> **2 tablespoons lemon juice**
> **2 teaspoons onion powder**
> **2 teaspoons garlic powder**

Variation:

> For a spicy sauce, add:
>
> **curry powder, to taste**

Yogurt-Cheese Sauce

Makes: 3-4 cups

A versatile sauce that doubles as a spread.

Preparation time: 20-25 minutes

Melt over low heat:
3 tablespoons butter

Add slowly, stirring constantly to keep mixture smooth:
2-3 tablespoons whole wheat pastry flour (depending on how thick a sauce you want)

Cook mixture for a few minutes over low flame, stirring occasionally. Meanwhile, heat over low flame until hot but not boiling:
1½ cups yogurt
½ teaspoon black pepper
pinch of cayenne

Add yogurt mixture to butter and flour a little at a time, whisking constantly. Cook until sauce is thoroughly heated. Add, a little at a time, whisking constantly:
2 cups (packed) grated, sharp cheddar cheese

After cheese melts, remove from heat and add:
3 thinly sliced green onions (including tops)
a few sautéed mushrooms (optional)

The mixture should be hot enough to cook the onions. Add onions sooner if more cooking is desired. Excellent over soufflés and steamed vegetables. Use cold as a spread for crackers.

Butter Sauce

Makes: ½ cup

A simple and delicious way to embellish vegetables.

Preparation time: 5 minutes

Melt:
¼ pound butter

Season with any of the following:
1 teaspoon turmeric
juice of 1 lemon with or without 1 tablespoon tamari
pressed garlic clove lightly sautéed in butter
1 teaspoon any dried herb or combination of herbs
2 teaspoons light miso

Tamari-Garlic Sauce

Makes: 4 cups

Preparation time: 8-10 minutes

Combine in large saucepan and whisk together until smooth:
⅓-½ cup tamari (depending on how strong a tamari flavor you want)
½ teaspoon black pepper
1 teaspoon garlic powder
1½ cups buttermilk
1½ cups sour cream
½ cup nutritional yeast

Cook over medium heat for 3-5 minutes or until heated through. Serve with noodles, millet or rice.

Sour Cream-
Mayonnaise Dip

Makes: a little over 2 cups

Preparation time: 15-20 minutes
Chilling time: overnight

Combine and mix well:

1 cup sour cream
1 cup mayonnaise
½ teaspoon salt
½ teaspoon paprika
3 tablespoons grated onion
¼ teaspoon curry powder
½ tablespoon lemon juice
¼ cup (packed) fresh minced parsley
1 large clove garlic, finely minced or pressed
½ teaspoon Worcestershire sauce

Chill overnight.

Variation:

Substitute for sour cream and mayonnaise:

2 cups yogurt

Spicy Avocado
Sandwich Spread

Makes: 2¾ cups

Preparation time: 15-20 minutes

Mash in medium bowl:
   5 large avocados

Add:
   2 tablespoons plus ½ teaspoon lemon juice
   1 tablespoon tamari or more, to taste
   6 small cloves garlic, pressed
   6 tablespoons plain yogurt
   4 tablespoons finely chopped green onions (including
      tops)
   ¾ teaspoon cumin powder or more, to taste
   ¾ teaspoon chile powder or more, to taste
   salt, to taste

Serve on bread with sprouts, thinly sliced cheese, and
raw mushrooms.

Artichoke-Olive
Sandwich Spread

Makes: 3 cups

Preparation time: 15-20 minutes

Cream with mixer:
   2 cups soft cream cheese (about 1 pound)

Add and stir in:

**two 6-ounce jars marinated artichoke hearts, drained
    and chopped (save oil)**
½ cup (packed) chopped black olives
1 teaspoon onion powder
1 rounded teaspoon oregano or more, to taste
6 tablespoons artichoke oil

Serve as a dip or sandwich spread.

Variation:

Instead of cream cheese use:

grated cheddar or Jack cheese

Eggplant Dip

Makes: 1½ cups

Preparation time: 20-30 minutes

Cut into ½-inch cubes and steam until soft:

1 medium eggplant

Mash the steamed eggplant and add:

½ cup yogurt
6 tablespoons sour cream
1 teaspoon salt
¼ teaspoon black pepper

Variation:

For a spicier dip add:

2 tablespoons tahini
4 cloves garlic, pressed
½ teaspoon coriander

Spicy Mid-Eastern Dip

Makes: 1 cup

Preparation time: 40 minutes

Peel and cut into ½-inch slices:

1 large eggplant

In a large skillet, sauté eggplant over medium heat until browned and very soft in:

4-6 tablespoons hot vegetable oil*

Drain on paper towels and set aside for 10 minutes. In large bowl, combine:

3 tablespoons peanut butter
3 tablespoons fresh lemon juice
2 cloves garlic, minced or pressed

Add cooled eggplant to mixture and blend with spoon or blender. Season with:

⅛ teaspoon salt

Drain off excess oil, if any. Excellent as a dip for pita bread, crackers or crisp vegetables.

Please note:

*The oil should be hot enough that the eggplant sizzles when placed in pan. Add more oil as needed.

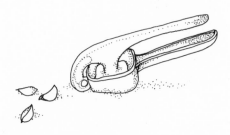

Guacamole

Makes: 1 cup

Preparation time: 10-15 minutes

In a medium bowl, mash:

1 large or 2 small avocados

Stir in:

1½ teaspoons freshly squeezed lemon juice
1 tablespoon finely minced green or white onion
⅛-¼ teaspoon salt
¼ teaspoon chile powder
¼ teaspoon cumin powder
1 green Ortega chile, chopped
1 clove garlic, minced or pressed
1 tablespoon sour cream
½ teaspoon chile salsa
pinch of coriander
1 small tomato, chopped (optional)

If you cover guacamole with plastic wrap, it will keep for 24 hours without discoloring. (Lay plastic directly onto guacamole.)

Yeast Gravy

Makes: 1 cup

Preparation time: 15-20 minutes

Melt in medium saucepan over medium heat:
   3 tablespoons butter

Sauté until soft and pale gold in color, adding
more butter if necessary:
   ½ cup chopped onions

Add and cook for 3 minutes:
   3 tablespoons whole wheat pastry flour
   2 tablespoons nutritional yeast (flaked variety)
   ¼ teaspoon thyme
   ¼ teaspoon savory
   ¼ teaspoon rounded garlic powder
   a pinch of marjoram
   ½ teaspoon tamari
   pinch of black pepper
   1 unsalted vegetable bouillon cube

Remove from heat and slowly whisk in, until smooth:
   1½ cups water

Return saucepan to heat and cook, stirring
continually until thick.

Cashew Gravy

Makes: 4 cups

Very rich.

Preparation time: 20-25 minutes

Sauté in large skillet over medium heat until golden:
6 tablespoons butter
1 medium onion, chopped

Stir in, cook for 3 minutes, stirring constantly:
6 tablespoons whole wheat pastry flour
1¼ cups finely ground raw cashews

Add slowly, whisking constantly until mixture is smooth:
3 unsalted vegetable bouillon cubes (dissolved in
4 cups boiling water)

Add:
5 tablespoons tamari
⅜ teaspoon garlic powder or more, to taste
black pepper, to taste

Bring gravy to a boil, then turn down heat and simmer until thick. Purée in blender in batches to ensure smoothness.

Variation:

Just before serving, add:
¼ cup chopped fresh parsley

Adjust the seasonings if necessary.

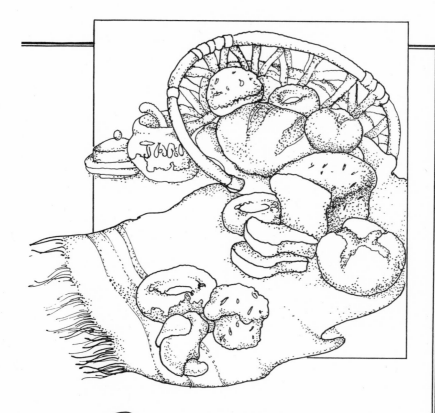

Quick Breads

Lemon Scones

Makes: 20-24 scones

Preparation time: 40 minutes
Baking time: 12-15 minutes

Preheat oven to 450°. Sift together in medium bowl:

4 cups whole wheat pastry flour
4 teaspoons baking powder
1½ teaspoons baking soda
1 teaspoon salt

Stir in:

3½ tablespoons lemon rind

Cut in with a knife or pastry cutter until mixture resembles coarse meal:

⅓ cup cold vegetable shortening
⅓ cup cold butter

Mix together:

1½ cups buttermilk
4 tablespoons honey

Make a well in the center of flour mixture and pour in sweetened buttermilk. Toss with fork until blended. Knead dough on floured board until smooth (3-5 times). Use flour as needed to keep dough from sticking to board. Roll dough out (adding flour as needed) to ½-inch thick. Cut into 2-inch to 2½-inch rounds. Arrange rounds on ungreased cookie sheet 1 inch apart. Brush tops with:

half and half

Bake at 450° for 12-15 minutes until golden. Serve immediately with butter and jam.

Whole Wheat Biscuits

Makes: 24 biscuits

Tender and flaky.

Preparation time: 15-20 minutes
Baking time: 8-10 minutes

Preheat oven to 450°. Sift together:

**3 cups whole wheat flour (for a lighter biscuit use
    half unbleached and half whole wheat flour)**
¾ teaspoon salt
1½ tablespoons baking powder

Cut in with a fork or pastry cutter until mixture resembles fine meal:

1½ cubes butter (¾ cup)

Mix together and stir in:

¾ cup milk
3 eggs, beaten

Shape dough into a ball and roll out on a floured board into a rectangle ½-inch thick. Fold dough into thirds, envelope style, overlapping the ends. Turn dough slightly (about ¼ turn) and roll out lengthwise. Repeat folding and rolling-out process 3 times. Cut dough with biscuit cutter, place biscuits on ungreased cookie sheet, and bake at 450° for 8-10 minutes.

Variation:

Stir in with milk and eggs:

¾-1 cup grated sharp cheddar cheese

Popovers

Makes: 1 dozen

Preparation time: 10 minutes
Baking time: 35 minutes

Preheat oven to 425°. Whisk together:

3 eggs, beaten
1 cup milk
2 tablespoons melted butter
1 teaspoon honey
½ teaspoon salt

Stir in until smooth:

1 cup whole wheat pastry flour

Fill buttered muffin tins or custard cups half-full. Bake in preheated oven at 425° for 15 minutes, then reduce heat to 350° and bake an additional 20 minutes. Do not open the oven door while baking. When done, turn off oven and pierce sides of popovers with a sharp knife to let moisture escape. Allow popovers to dry in oven for 10 minutes. Popovers are best when served immediately.

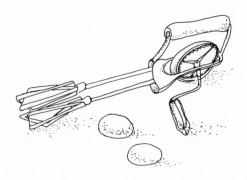

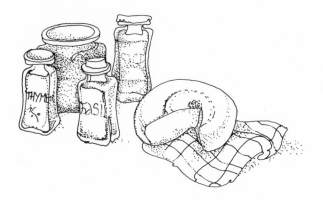

Herb-Cheese Popovers

Makes: 1 dozen

Preparation time: 15 minutes
Baking time: 35-40 minutes

Preheat oven to 425°. Follow the basic popover recipe, eliminating the honey and adding, after stirring in flour:

½ **cup grated sharp cheddar cheese**
pinch of cayenne
½ **teaspoon thyme**
¼ **teaspoon sage**
¼ **teaspoon basil**
¼ **teaspoon paprika**

Follow the same baking procedure as with plain popovers, but bake an additional 5 minutes at 350°.

These popovers are not as light as plain popovers—they have more of a muffin consistency.

Gruyère Classique

A puffed moist cheese bread, to serve with soup, salad, as an appetizer, or with brunch.

Preparation time: 25 minutes
Baking time: 40 minutes

Preheat oven to 400°. Bring to a boil in medium saucepan:

1 cup water
½ cup butter
½ teaspoon salt

Stir in, mixing thoroughly until dough forms a ball in the center:

2 cups whole wheat pastry flour

Remove from heat, allow to cool for a few minutes, then beat in, 2 at a time, mixing thoroughly:

4 large eggs

Set aside to cool. Then add and mix well:

1 cup (packed) grated Gruyère cheese
large pinch of cayenne

On a buttered baking sheet, form dough into a large circle about 8 inches in diameter with a 3-inch hole in the center. Bake at 400° for 10 minutes, then reduce heat to 350° and bake 25 to 30 minutes longer or until ring becomes puffed, dry, and golden brown.

Chappatis

Preparation time: 20-25 minutes
Cooking time: 45 minutes

Combine in medium bowl:

2 cups whole wheat flour
1 teaspoon salt

Add gradually until a soft dough is formed:

¾-1 cup water

Knead until dough is very pliable. Cover with a damp cloth and let sit for 10-15 minutes. Lightly grease and heat a frying pan, preferably cast-iron. Knead dough once more and break off walnut-size balls. Flatten balls between fingers, dip in flour and roll out evenly and thinly on a floured board. Heat briefly on one side until the edges curl. Turn over and press edges with spatula as bubbles begin to form. The perfect chappati will balloon completely (but don't worry if it doesn't!). Remove from pan and brush lightly with butter. The chappati must be fried quickly or it will turn hard.

Another method of cooking chappatis is to heat lightly on both sides in a frying pan, then place already-fried chappati over medium flame for a few minutes, turning quickly.

Variation:

For a lighter chappati, use:

1 cup whole wheat flour
1 cup unbleached flour

Whole Wheat Cranberry Orange-Nut Bread

Makes: 1 loaf

A good make-ahead holiday bread.

Preparation time: 30 minutes
Baking time: 1 hour and 15 minutes

Preheat oven to 350°. Mix together in medium bowl and let stand:

1½ cups cranberries, coarsely chopped (to save time, chop by using quick on and off motion with blender or food processor)
¾ cup honey

Grate the rind and then juice:

3 medium juice oranges

You should have 3 tablespoons of orange rind. Set rind aside. Mix orange juice and cranberry-honey mixture. Add:

1 egg, beaten
5 tablespoons melted butter

Sift together:

1¾ cups whole wheat pastry flour
4 teaspoons baking powder
¾ teaspoon baking soda

Add:

3 tablespoons grated orange rind

Combine liquid with dry ingredients. Stir in:

1 cup coarsely chopped walnuts

Spoon mixture into buttered loaf pan. Bake at 350° for 1 hour and 15 minutes. Start checking after 1 hour. Bread is done when a toothpick inserted in the center comes out clean. Cool in the pan or on a wire rack for 10 minutes. Then turn out of the pan and cool completely. Wrap in aluminum foil and refrigerate until the next day (optional).

Please note:

This bread is best served the day after baking.

Applesauce Cornbread

Serves: 8-10

Moist and chewy. Good for breakfast or as a tea bread.

Preparation time: 20 minutes
Baking time: 40 minutes

Preheat oven to 350°. Combine in medium bowl:

2 cups whole wheat pastry flour
1 cup cornmeal
¾ teaspoon salt

Combine in separate bowl:

1 teaspoon baking soda
1 cup buttermilk
⅔ cup honey

Combine wet and dry ingredients. Add:

¾ cup unsweetened applesauce
1 cup raisins

Stir just enough to moisten dry ingredients. Spoon into a well-buttered 8-inch square pan and bake at 350° for 40 minutes.

Pumpkin
or Squash Cornbread

Serves: 6-10

Sweet and moist.

Preparation time: 20 minutes
Baking time: 1½ hours

Preheat oven to 350°. Cream in medium bowl:
½ cup soft butter
¾ cup honey

Add and mix well:

2 eggs, beaten
1½ cups cooked mashed pumpkin or winter squash
(canned works well)
1 cup milk

Combine in separate bowl:

1½ cups whole wheat pastry flour or whole wheat
flour
1 cup cornmeal
1 tablespoon plus 2 teaspoons baking powder
1 teaspoon cinnamon
¼ teaspoon allspice
½ teaspoon salt
⅛ teaspoon powdered ginger

Add dry ingredients to the pumpkin or squash mixture
and mix thoroughly. Spoon mixture into large, buttered
loaf pan, filling it ¾ full*. Bake at 350° for 1½ hours.
(Check after 1 hour to see if done. If top browns too
quickly, cover with aluminum foil.)

Please note:

*Use left-over batter to make muffins. Bake in greased
and floured tins (or tins lined with paper cupcake liners)
at 350° for 15-20 minutes or until done.

Sweet
Cornbread or Muffins

Serves: 6-9

Preparation time: 15 minutes
Baking time: 25 minutes for cornbread, 15-20 minutes for muffins

Preheat oven to 350°. Blend in medium-large bowl and set aside:

½ cup safflower or other light vegetable oil
½ cup honey
2-3 eggs, beaten (3 eggs make the bread more cake-like)

Sift together in medium bowl:

1½ cups whole wheat pastry flour
1 tablespoon baking powder
⅛ teaspoon salt

Mix in with the flour:

1½ cups yellow corn meal

Mix dry ingredients with egg mixture, gradually adding:

1 cup milk

For bread:

Pour into greased and floured 8-inch square pan and sprinkle with:

1 tablespoon poppy seeds

Bake 25 minutes or until done.

For muffins:

Grease muffin tins or use paper cupcake liners. Mixture will make 18-20 average size muffins. Bake at 350° for 15-20 minutes or until done.

Orange-Prune Tea Bread

Makes: 1 loaf

Preparation time: 30-35 minutes
Baking time: 1½ hours
Chilling time: overnight

Preheat oven to 300°. Wash and put through food grinder, using fine blade:

1 medium orange, unpeeled

Boil:

½ cup water

Pour water over:

1 cup(packed) pitted and coarsely chopped dried prunes (use vacuum-packed, pitted variety)

Add to water and let stand:

1½ teaspoons baking soda

Cream together:

1 tablespoon melted butter
⅔ cup honey
1 egg
1 teaspoon vanilla

Sift together:

2½ cups whole wheat pastry flour
1 tablespoon baking powder
½ teaspoon salt

Add dry ingredients to creamed mixture, alternating ground orange with water from the prunes. Stir in prunes and:

1 cup chopped nuts

Spoon mixture into buttered loaf pan. Bake at 300° for 1½ hours or until a toothpick inserted in center comes out clean. Cool in pan for 10 minutes. Remove from pan, cool completely, wrap in aluminum foil and refrigerate overnight.

Quick Oat Bread

Makes: 1 loaf

A sweet, moist bread with a chewy crust.

Preparation time: 15-20 minutes
Baking time: a little over 1 hour

Preheat oven to 350°. Boil for 5 minutes in medium saucepan:

1 cup raisins
1 cup water

Meanwhile, combine in medium bowl:

1 cup oats
1 cup whole wheat pastry flour
1 cup bran
½ teaspoon salt
1 teaspoon cinnamon
¼ teaspoon nutmeg

Mix in separate bowl:

1 cup buttermilk
1 teaspoon baking soda
½ cup honey

Combine wet and dry ingredients, add raisin mixture, and stir only until dry ingredients are moistened. Spoon mixture into buttered loaf pan and bake at 350° for a little over 1 hour. Cool in the pan and then on a cooling rack for 10 minutes. Serve warm or at room temperature.

Spiced Apple Muffins

Makes: 24 muffins

Preparation time: 30 minutes
Baking time: 15 minutes

Preheat oven to 400°. Combine in medium bowl:

1 cup honey
1 cup safflower oil
4 eggs, beaten

Combine in separate bowl:

2½ cups whole wheat pastry flour
2 teaspoons baking powder
½ teaspoon salt
½ cup non-instant milk powder
½ teaspoon allspice
¾ teaspoon nutmeg
2 teaspoons cinnamon

Combine dry and wet ingredients and mix well. Stir in:

2 large apples, peeled, cored, and grated
1½ teaspoons vanilla
¾ cup chopped walnuts
¾ cup raisins

Bake at 400° for 15 minutes in buttered muffin tins.

Carrot Bran Muffins

Makes: 24 muffins

Moist and light.

Preparation time: 20 minutes
Baking time: 20 minutes

Preheat oven to 375°. Combine in medium bowl:

 1½ cups whole wheat pastry flour
 ¾ teaspoon salt
 1½ teaspoons baking soda
 1½ cups bran
 1 teaspoon cinnamon
 ½ teaspoon nutmeg

Combine in large bowl:

 1½ cups milk
 2 tablespoons apple cider vinegar
 ⅓ cup honey
 ¼ cup molasses
 1 cup (packed) grated carrots
 2 eggs, beaten
 ¼ cup safflower oil
 ¾ cup raisins
 ½ cup chopped walnuts

Combine wet and dry ingredients. Mix just enough to moisten dry ingredients. Fill buttered muffin tins ⅔ full and bake at 375° for 20 minutes.

Desserts

Rhubarb Fool

Serves: 8-10

A rich yet delicate dessert.

Preparation time: 15-20 minutes
Cooking time: 10-15 minutes
Chilling time: 30 minutes

Steam until soft (about 10-15 minutes):

**2 pounds trimmed rhubarb (about 7 large stalks),
diced**

Place rhubarb in large bowl or serving dish. Add:

**¾ cup honey
⅛ teaspoon cinnamon
pinch of nutmeg
pinch of cardamon
pinch of cloves**

Mix well, then chill. Whip:

½ pint heavy cream

Blend whipped cream with chilled rhubarb mixture. Garnish with:

fresh mint leaves or strawberries

Pecan Shortbread Cookies

Makes: approx 2 1/2 doz

Preparation time: 25-30 minutes
Baking time: 15-20 minutes per batch

Preheat oven to 325°. Cream together until fluffy:
1 cup butter, softened
$^1/_2$ cup sugar
2 teaspoons vanilla extract

Sift together, then add to the creamed mixture, blending well:
$1^3/_4$ cups flour
$^1/_4$ teaspoon salt
$^1/_4$ teaspoon cardamom

Add, mixing well (you may need to use your hands):
$1^1/_2$ cups finely chopped pecans (walnuts or hazelnuts may be substituted)

Shape the dough into 1-inch balls and place on an ungreased cookie sheet about 2 inches apart. Bake 15-20 minutes. Remove to a cooling rack. When cool roll each cookie in a mixture of:
$^1/_3$ cup powdered sugar
$^1/_8$ teaspoon cardamom

Store in an airtight container.

Honey Custard

Makes: 10 servings

Delicious served warm or cold. Try topping it
with our Honey Nut Sauce for a special occasion.

Preparation time: 15 minutes
Baking time: 25-40 minutes

Preheat oven to 350°. Scald in a medium pan:
   3 cups half 'n half (you can use all milk if you
      wish)
   3 cups milk

While milk is heating, butter custard cups or large
oven-proof dish (not aluminum). A 10-inch Pyrex
dish works perfectly. When milk is hot remove from
heat and whisk in:

   1 cup clover honey (or other light honey)

In a large bowl beat well:

   8 eggs
   1 Tablespoon vanilla extract

Very slowly add a little of the hot milk to the eggs,
whisking constantly. Continue adding the milk a
little at a time as the temperature of the raw eggs is
slowly raised. Once half the milk is added you can
pour in remainder. Add, if desired:

   3 cups raspberries or other berries—even in
   combination (fruit is optional)

Pour into buttered cups or dish and place in a pan
with very hot water, which comes about 1 inch up the
sides of the custard dish. Carefully set in oven and
bake until it tests done—about 25 minutes for
custard cups and 40 minutes for a large dish. It will
still look very liquidy, but insert a knife near the
center. If it comes out clean your custard is done. If
overcooked, custard separates and will have watery
areas—but still tastes fine.

Pineapple Mousse

Serves: 8

Preparation time: 25 minutes
Chilling time: 3 hours

Cut lengthwise:
  1 ripe pineapple

Scoop out fruit from both halves, removing the core.
Finely chop the fruit, reserving juice. Mix pineapple
with:

  1½ tablespoons lime juice
  ½ cup honey
  2 cups heavy cream, whipped

Spoon mixture into an 8-inch square pan. Place in
freezer for approximately 3 hours or until slightly firm.
(To make this dish ahead of time, freeze the pineapple
mixture solid and then remove from freezer 20 minutes
before serving to allow it to soften.) Serve garnished
with:

  slices of kiwi and sprigs of fresh mint

Trailmix Cookies

Makes: 4 dozen

Preparation time: 25-30 minutes
Baking time: 15-20 minutes

Preheat oven to 350°. Blend thoroughly in large bowl:

**1½ cups honey or more, to taste (adding more honey
   will make cookies more moist and chewy)
1½ cups safflower oil
2 eggs, beaten**

Sift together and add to honey mixture:

**4 cups whole wheat pastry flour
2 teaspoons salt
2 tablespoons cinnamon
1 teaspoon baking soda**

Stir in:

**4 cups rolled oats
5 teaspoons vanilla
½ cup chopped walnuts
½ cup chopped almonds
½ cup chopped cashews
1 cup fine unsweetened coconut
1 cup raisins
1 cup chopped dates
1¾ cups unsweetened carob chips**

Drop by large spoonfuls onto lightly greased cookie
sheet. Bake at 350° for 15-20 minutes.

Maple Walnut Pie

A holiday favorite!

Preparation time: 30 minutes, including crust
Baking time: 30 minutes

Preheat oven at 375°. Then melt in a 2-quart sauce-pan:

$^1/_2$ **cup butter**
$^1/_2$ **cup honey**
$^3/_4$ **cup brown sugar**
$^1/_4$ **cup maple syrup**

Turn off heat.

Beat three eggs and add slowly to above. While whisking quickly, add:

1 teaspoon vanilla
$^1/_2$ **teaspoon salt**
2 cups chopped walnuts

Pour into partially baked pie shell and bake 30 minutes at 375°. Cool.

Serve with vanilla ice cream or sweetened whipped cream.

Orange-Pineapple Sherbet

Serves: 6

Preparation time: 25-30 minutes
Chilling time: 3 hours

Combine and freeze until firm:

**two 20-ounce cans unsweetened pineapple chunks
(drain chunks well)
5 medium oranges, peeled and cut into chunks
2 tablespoons triple sec (orange liqueur)
1 cup plain yogurt
½ cup honey**

After mixture freezes, cut into chunks and put through a
Champion juicer. Serve immediately or refreeze. Allow
sherbet to soften before serving. Garnish with any
combination of the following:

**mandarin orange sections
sliced kiwi fruit
fresh mint**

Orange-Pumpkin Pudding

Serves: 8-10

Preparation time: 20-25 minutes
Baking time: 50 minutes

Preheat oven to 350°. Combine in large bowl (a whisk works best) and pour into a buttered 2½-quart baking dish:

2½ cups cooked and mashed pumpkin
3 eggs, beaten
scant cup honey
½ teaspoon salt
½ teaspoon allspice
2½ teaspoons cinnamon
¾ teaspoon ground cloves
2 rounded tablespoons grated orange rind
1 cup milk
1 cup half and half
scant cup non-instant powdered milk
1 cup finely chopped walnuts

Bake at 350° for 50 minutes or until knife inserted in center comes out clean. Serve warm or cold with:

whipped cream

Lemon Sponge Custard

Serves: 4-6

Preparation time: 20 minutes
Baking time: 40-50 minutes
Chilling time: 1 hour

Preheat oven to 350°. Cream in medium bowl:

½ cup honey
1½ tablespoons soft butter
2 rounded teaspoons lemon rind
7 egg yolks

Stir in and whisk together:

4 tablespoons whole wheat pastry flour
¼ cup plus 1 tablespoon fresh lemon juice
1 cup milk

Fold in:

7 stiffly beaten egg whites

Pour into custard cups or 8-inch square baking dish and place in a large pan filled with hot water reaching ⅔ up the side of cups or dish. Bake for 40-50 minutes at 350° or until knife inserted in center comes out clean.
Remove custard cups from hot water at once and chill.

Raspberry Torte

Serves: 12

A honey version of Linzertorte.

Preparation time: 40-45 minutes
Baking time: 45-50 minutes
Chilling time: 6 hours

Preheat oven to 350°. Mix together in large bowl:

1½ cups whole wheat pastry flour
2 teaspoons lemon rind
1½ teaspoons orange rind
⅛ teaspoon salt
1 rounded tablespoon cinnamon
¾ teaspoon ground cloves

Cut in until mixture resembles coarse meal:

1 cup cold butter

Stir in and mix well:

⅓ cup plus 2 tablespoons honey
2 egg yolks, beaten
1½ cups ground almonds

Press ⅔ of the dough into a 9-inch *deep* quiche or tart pan, until dough reaches halfway up the sides. Chill until firm. Mix together and spoon onto chilled crust:

1½ cups seedless honey raspberry jam
½ cup unsweetened apple sauce

Using a pastry bag, pipe remaining dough onto jam in lattice pattern. If pastry bag is not available, chill dough very well, roll out between waxed paper, cut into strips and lay lattice-fashion on top of jam. Bake at 350° for 45-50 minutes. Cover with foil if top starts to get brown. Chill thoroughly (6 hours) before serving. Cut in thin wedges and serve with:

unsweetened or lightly sweetened whipped cream

Apple-Custard Tart

Serves: 12

Preparation time: 45-50 minutes
Baking time: 1 hour and 45 minutes
Chilling time: 30-35 minutes

Preheat oven to 400°. To make crust, mix together:

2 cups whole wheat pastry flour
⅛ teaspoon salt
1 tablespoon grated lemon rind

Cut in and blend until mixture resembles coarse meal:

1½ cubes cold butter (¾ cup)

Stir in:

⅓ cup honey
1 egg yolk
2 teaspoons vanilla
1 cup ground almonds

Press dough into an 11-inch springform pan. Dough should reach ¾ up the sides. Sprinkle over crust:

½ cup ground almonds

Chill until firm (30-35 minutes). In the meantime, soak and set aside:

½ cup currants in
3½ tablespoons brandy

In a large bowl, combine:

7 large golden delicious apples, peeled, cored and
**   sliced**
1 tablespoon lemon juice
2 teaspoons cinnamon
¼ cup honey

Spoon mixture into chilled crust and bake at 400° for 25 minutes. (Cover with foil after 7 minutes.) Remove from oven and reduce temperature to 350°.

To make custard, mix together with the soaked currants (including brandy):

4 eggs, beaten
1½ cups half and half
⅓ cup honey
pinch of salt
1 teaspoon vanilla

Pour over apples, evenly distributing currants. Bake at 350° for 1 hour and 15 minutes or until knife inserted in center comes out clean. Cool slightly before removing rim. Serve chilled or at room temperature.

Halva

Makes 16-20 pieces

Preparation time: 25 minutes

Heat together in medium saucepan over medium heat:

1½ cups water
1½ cups milk
1½ cups honey
1½ cups raisins

In a large saucepan, melt:

1½ cubes butter (¾ cup)

Add:

1½ cups almonds or pine nuts, coarsely chopped
1½ cups Farina or cream of wheat (non-instant)

Stir over low heat to brown the nuts and toast the cream of wheat. Then add hot milk mixture a little at a time, stirring until thick. Spoon mixture into buttered 9-inch square pan. Let it set until firm. Cut into pieces.

Tender Whole Wheat
Pie Crust

Makes: a single 9-inch pie crust

Preparation time: 15 minutes
Baking time: 8-10 minutes

Preheat oven to 400°. Place in bowl of food processor:
  ³/₄ cup unbleached white flour
  ³/₄ cup whole wheat flour (*not* whole wheat pastry flour)
  1 stick cold butter, cut in large pieces

Turn on food processor* adding 1 tablespoon water at a time until it forms a ball:

approximately 3 tablespoons cold water

Roll out on lightly floured board. Place in a 9-inch pie plate. Flute the edges and prick bottom and sides with a fork. Bake at 400° for 8-10 minutes for pies that call for pre-baked crusts.

*If you don't have a processor, a quick way to mix the dough is to grate the butter through a hand grater into the bowl of flours.

Sweet
Pastry Crust

Makes: a single 9-inch pie crust

Preparation time: 27 minutes

Preheat oven to 425°. Sift together in medium bowl:
1¼ cups whole wheat pastry flour
⅛ teaspoon salt
½ rounded teaspoon baking powder

Add and stir in:
½-1 teaspoon grated lemon rind
2 tablespoons finely ground almonds

Cut in with a pastry blender until mixture resembles
coarse meal:
½ cup cold butter

Add and mix well:
2 tablespoons honey
1 tablespoon brandy

Press into 9-inch pie plate. Bake at 425° for 7 minutes.
Cover edges with aluminum foil to prevent them from
getting too dark. Cool and fill with your favorite filling.

Fruit Shortcake

Serves: 8-9

Preparation time: 45 minutes

Blackberry:

Combine in large saucepan:

2 pounds unsweetened blackberries, fresh or frozen
½ cup honey
4 tablespoons butter
1 cup apple-berry juice

Mix separately:

4 tablespoons cornstarch
½ cup apple-berry juice

Add cornstarch mixture to saucepan and bring to a boil. Cook over low heat until thickened. Remove from heat and add:

1 teaspoon lemon juice

This filling, and the others, will thicken more as they cool.

Blueberry:

Follow the same procedure as above, using the following ingredients:

2 pounds blueberries, fresh or frozen
1½ cups apple-berry juice
½ cup honey
4 tablespoons butter
3½ tablespoons cornstarch
1 teaspoon lemon juice

Cherry:

Follow the same procedure as above, using the following ingredients:

> 2 pounds dark sweet cherries, fresh or frozen
> 1½ cups cherry cider
> ⅓ cup honey
> 4 tablespoons butter
> 2 tablespoons cornstarch
> 1 teaspoon lemon juice

While filling cools, prepare:

Shortcake Biscuits:

Sift together:

> 1½ cups whole wheat pastry flour
> pinch of salt
> 2 teaspoons baking powder

Stir in:

> ½ teaspoon grated lemon rind (optional)

Cut in with a knife or pastry cutter, until mixture resembles coarse meal:

> 4 tablespoons butter

Mix together and add to flour:

> ½ cup milk
> 1 tablespoon honey

Stir well. Knead on floured board until dough is smooth—about 30 seconds. Roll dough out to ½-inch thickness. Cut biscuits out with biscuit cutter or a glass. Place biscuits on ungreased cookie sheet and bake at 375° for 10-12 minutes or until golden brown.

To serve, slice biscuits in half, spoon some of the filling on top, cover with the other half of the biscuit, and top with more filling. Delicious with whipped cream or ice cream.

Please note:

These fillings are excellent in pies.

Crunchy Honey Fruit Crisp

Serves: 6

Preparation time: 40-45 minutes
Baking time: 50 minutes

Preheat oven to 350°.

Crust:

Combine and mix well:
3 tablespoons whole wheat pastry flour
1½ cups rolled oats
½ cup finely chopped pecans
2 teaspoons cinnamon

Melt together and add to flour mixture:
6 tablespoons butter
½ cup honey

For apple crisp:

Mix together in large bowl:
8 large cooking apples, peeled, cored and thinly
  sliced
¼ cup honey
3 teaspoons fresh lemon juice
2 teaspoons cinnamon

Spoon apple mixture into 9-inch square buttered baking
dish, pressing apples down. (Dish will be very full.) Top
with oat mixture. Bake at 350° for 50 minutes. If the
topping starts to get too brown, cover with aluminum
foil. Crisp is done when apples feel tender when pierced
with a fork.

For peach crisp:

Combine:

2 pounds fresh or frozen unsweetened peaches, sliced
¼ teaspoon almond extract
2 tablespoons fresh lemon juice

Heat until melted and mix with peaches:

½ cup honey or, to taste
3 tablespoons butter

Follow baking instructions for apple crisp. Serve at room temperature, topped with:

whipped cream or ice cream

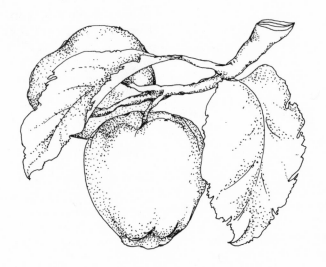

Strawberry Pie

Serves: 6-8

Preparation time: 35 minutes
Chilling time: 1 hour

To make crust, use Sweet Pastry Crust recipe (page 191).
To make filling, arrange points up on bottom of cooled
pastry crust:

1 large basket strawberries

Blend in blender:

2 small baskets strawberries
⅓ cup honey
1 tablespoon lemon juice
2½ tablespoons cornstarch

Cook strawberry mixture in medium saucepan over low
heat, stirring constantly for 15 minutes or until mixture
turns dark red. Place pan with strawberry mixture in cold
running water, stirring until almost cool. Pour mixture
over strawberries in pie pan. Refrigerate. Decorate pie
with:

lightly sweetened whipped cream

Strawberry Cake

Serves: 10-12

An elegant strawberry dish.

Preparation time: 1 hour 15 minutes
Baking time: 35 minutes

Preheat oven to 350°. Butter and flour two 8-inch cake
pans. Cream in large bowl:

⅔ cup softened butter
1 cup honey
1¼ teaspoons vanilla
**4 egg yolks (set aside egg whites at room tempera-
    ture)**

Sift together:

2½ cups whole wheat pastry flour
1 tablespoon baking powder
½ teaspoon salt

Starting and ending with dry ingredients, add dry ingredients to butter mixture, alternating with:

1¼ cups milk

Beat until stiff and fold into batter:

4 egg whites

Pour batter into pans and bake at 350° for 30-35 minutes
or until toothpick inserted in center comes out clean.
Cool for 5 minutes in pan, then turn out onto cooling

racks. When completely cool, slice each layer in half, horizontally, creating four layers. Prepare:

4 cups sliced strawberries (2 small baskets)
6 tablespoons finely chopped almonds, or ¼ cup almonds ground in blender

Whip until stiff:

2 cups whipping cream

Add:

2 tablespoons honey
1 teaspoon vanilla or 1½ teaspoons Grand Marnier or, to taste

To assemble:

Place one layer of cake, cut side up, on cake plate. Spread ¼ of the whipped cream on top. Cover completely with 1 cup strawberries. Sprinkle with 1½ tablespoons almonds. Repeat procedure with remaining layers except for top layer. Cover top layer with whipped cream, placing an extra dollop in the center. Surround with strawberries. Sprinkle with nuts.

Variation:

For added sweetness, spread thinly over the first three layers before topping with whipped cream:

strawberry jam

Orange-Date Cake

Serves: 12

Rich and moist.

Preparation time: 35-40 minutes
Baking time: 1 hour and 15 minutes

Preheat oven to 350°. In a large bowl, combine and soak:

   1 cup boiling water
   2 cups (packed) chopped dates
   ·1½ teaspoons baking soda

When the water cools, add and set aside:

   ½ cup freshly squeezed orange juice

Cream together in large bowl:

   1 cup butter
   1 cup honey
   4 eggs, beaten
   1 teaspoon vanilla

Combine and add to creamed mixture:

   2¼ cups whole wheat pastry flour
   1 teaspoon salt
   1 teaspoon cinnamon

Stir in soaked dates and:

   grated rind of 1½ medium oranges
   1 cup chopped walnuts

Spoon into buttered and floured bundt or tube pan. Bake at 350° for 1 hour and 15 minutes or until a toothpick inserted in center comes out clean. Do not frost—serve with:

   unsweetened whipped cream

Lazy Daisy Oatmeal Cake

Serves: 8-10

Preparation time: 30 minutes
Baking time: 40-50 minutes

Preheat oven to 350°. Soak in medium bowl for 20 minutes and set aside to cool:

1 cup rolled oats
1¼ cups boiling water

Cream until light:

½ cup butter or margarine
1 cup honey

Beat in:

2 eggs
1 teaspoon vanilla

Set mixture aside. Sift:

1½ cups whole wheat pastry flour

Sift flour again, this time combined with:

1 teaspoon baking soda
½ teaspoon salt
¾ teaspoon cinnamon
¼ teaspoon nutmeg

Stir cooled soaked oats into creamed mixture. Add flour and mix well. Spoon into buttered and floured 8-inch square pan and bake at 350° for 40-50 minutes. Frost with Frosting for Lazy Daisy Oatmeal Cake (opposite page).

Frosting for Lazy Daisy Oatmeal Cake

Preparation time: 10 minutes

Preheat boiler. Combine:

½ cup butter or margarine (room temperature)
1 cup honey
6 tablespoons cream or milk
1½ cups finely flaked unsweetened coconut
⅔ cup chopped nuts

While cake is still hot, spread with frosting and put under preheated broiler until bubbly and tinged with gold. Watch closely, as frosting burns easily. Cool. Serve with:

whipped cream

Upside-Down Plum Cake

Serves: 8

Preparation time: 30-40 minutes
Baking time: 35-40 minutes

Preheat oven to 400°. Combine:
> 1¼ cups whole wheat pastry flour
> 1 teaspoon baking powder
> pinch of salt

Add and mix well:
> ⅓ cup honey
> 3 egg yolks, beaten
> 1 tablespoon melted butter
> ¼ cup milk

In a separate bowl, toss:
> 2 cups halved ripe purple plums
> 1 tablespoon lemon juice
> 1 teaspoon grated lemon rind

Melt, thin if necessary with 1 tablespoon water, and press through a sieve:
> ¼ cup elderberry jelly or jam

Butter an 8-inch or 9-inch square pan. Pour melted jam on the bottom and dot with:
> 3 tablespoons butter

Drizzle over butter:
> ¼ cup honey

Drain plums and arrange halves on top of honey, cut side up. Pour batter over plums. Bake at 400° for 35-45 minutes. If the top starts to get too dark, cover with aluminum foil. Cool the cake in pan, then invert onto serving platter. Sprinkle with:

chopped toasted almonds

Serve with:

whipped cream

Apple Cake   Serves: 10-12

Preparation time: 25 minutes
Baking time: 45 minutes - 1 hour

Preheat oven to 350°. Cream in large bowl until fluffy:

3 eggs
1¼ cups honey
1 cup safflower oil
2 teaspoons vanilla
½ teaspoon nutmeg
1 tablespoon cinnamon
1 teaspoon baking soda
¼ teaspoon salt

Add and stir until thoroughly mixed:

2 cups whole wheat pastry flour

Fold in:

4 cups diced apples
1 cup chopped nuts

Spoon mixture into buttered 9-inch by 13-inch pan and bake at 350° for 45 minutes to 1 hour.

Lemon Loaf

Serves: 8-10

Slightly tart.

Preparation time: 25 minutes
Sitting time: 20 minutes
Baking time: 1 hour
Chilling time: 2-3 hours

Preheat oven to 325°. Mix together in large bowl until smooth and creamy:

2 tablespoons butter
½ cup honey
2 large eggs, beaten
½ cup milk

Sift together:

1½ cups whole wheat pastry flour
1 teaspoon baking powder
½ teaspoon salt

Slowly add dry ingredients to creamed mixture, mix well, then add:

1 rounded teaspoon grated lemon rind
2 tablespoons lemon juice
½ cup chopped walnuts

Spoon into standard-size buttered loaf pan and let sit in a warm spot for 20 minutes. Bake at 325°-350° for 1 hour. Cool for 10 minutes in pan, then turn out onto a cooling rack for 10 minutes. Place loaf on a plate. Perforate top by punching holes with a fork. Spoon onto top of loaf a mixture of:

2 tablespoons lemon juice
3 tablespoons honey

Allow loaf to absorb the juice. Chill for 2-3 hours. Slice very thin.

Lemon-Sesame Cake

Serves: 8-9

A uniquely flavored snack cake.

Preparation time: 15-20 minutes
Baking time: 30 minutes

Preheat oven to 350°. Cream together:
½ cup butter (room temperature)
½ cup tahini
2 teaspoons sesame oil
1 cup honey
3 eggs, beaten
1 teaspoon vanilla

Sift together and add to creamed mixture:
2¼ cups whole wheat pastry flour
1 teaspoon baking powder
½ teaspoon baking soda
½ teaspoon salt

Stir in:
1 tablespoon lemon rind
⅓ cup lemon juice
3 tablespoons toasted sesame seeds

Spoon mixture into buttered 8-inch or 9-inch square
pan. Sprinkle top with:
2 tablespoons raw sesame seeds

Bake at 350° for 30 minutes or until toothpick inserted
in center comes out clean. Cover with aluminum foil if
top starts to brown too quickly. It's best to eat this cake
the day it's made.

French Dessert Crêpes

Makes: 15-20 crêpes

An elegant dessert for entertaining. Can be made days in advance.

Preparation time: batter 15 minutes
　　　　　　　　　cooking 35 minutes
　　　　　　　　　filling 15 minutes

The crêpe batter:

In medium bowl sift together:
1 ³/₄ cups sifted unbleached flour
scant ¹/₂ cup superfine sugar
pinch of salt

Add, beating in one at a time:
4 whole eggs, room temperature
2 egg yolks

Add, using a wire whisk just until blended:
1¹/₂ cups whole milk
1 tablespoon cognac
¹/₂ teaspoon vanilla

Let stand at room temperature for ¹/₂ hour.

To cook crêpes:

Have ready:
¹/₂ stick butter for buttering pan

Warm a 7" crêpe pan or skillet over medium heat. Pour
batter into a measuring cup for ease of handling. Quickly
rub pan with butter using a paper towel. Pour ¹/₄ cup batter
(or less if you're experienced) into heated pan, rotating the
pan to allow the batter to cover entire bottom. Let crêpe
cook until completely dry on top. It will be slightly golden
around the edges. Run a spatula or knife around the edge to
loosen. Turn and cook for 5-10 seconds. Cool on a rack.

Butter the pan lightly before cooking each crêpe. When cool, they can be stacked with layers of waxed paper between each crêpe. Continue cooking until you have used up all the batter.

Fill each crêpe with:
> **high quality vanilla ice cream (One pint fills 6 crêpes.)**

Put ice cream in a tube shape across the center of each crêpe and roll. Be sure the ice cream goes clear to the ends. A dinner knife will help "cut pieces" of the ice cream. Place seam side down in a freezer-proof dish. Cover and freeze until ready to serve.

Top with your choice of the following variations:

I.   **"A Classic" Chocolate Sauce (p.212)**
> **whipped cream, lightly sweetened with a touch of creme de cacao ($^{1}/_{2}$ pint whipping cream, when whipped, will cover about 16 crêpes.)**
> **toasted hazelnuts or slivered almonds**

II.   **Fresh strawberries sliced and chilled with Grand Marnier (One regular-sized basket tops 7 crêpes.) Add 2 teaspoons Grand Marnier per basket, and refrigerate 1-3 hours.**
> **whipped cream, lightly sweetened**
> **toasted almonds**

III.   **A tropical version**
> **Pour 1 tablespoon coconut cream over each crêpe. (It comes sweetened.)**
> **Top with fresh chopped mango (4 for 18-20 crêpes) and a splash of light rum.**

Lemon-
Cream Cheese Chiffon Pie

Serves: 6-8

Preparation time: 45-50 minutes
Chilling time: 2-3 hours

Preheat oven to 375°.

Crust:

To make lemon cookie pie crust, mix thoroughly:

**1½ cups crushed lemon cookie crumbs (we prefer
the Healthway brand which contains only honey.
If you use a different brand, you may need to add
more lemon rind.)**
¾ teaspoon grated lemon rind
3 tablespoons butter, melted

Press mixture into pie pan and bake at 375° for
5 minutes, then chill.

Filling:

Combine in blender:

1 cup cottage cheese
8 ounces cream cheese, softened
¼ cup milk
½ cup plus 2 tablespoons honey
4½ tablespoons lemon juice
pinch of salt
2 rounded teaspoons grated lemon rind

Combine, let sit for 5 minutes, then bring to a boil:

2 teaspoons unflavored gelatin*
¼ cup cold water

Mix gelatin and cheese mixture together. Whip and fold
into above mixture:

½ pint unsweetened heavy whipping cream

Fold in:

1 cup thick plain yogurt

Spoon mixture into chilled crust. Refrigerate for 2-3 hours or until set. Garnish with:

fresh fruit (we prefer kiwi or strawberries)

Please note:

*Gelatin is an animal by-product.

Pumpkin Cheesecake   Serves: 6-8

Preparation time: 40-45 minutes (including crust)
Baking time: 40 minutes
Cooling time: 1 hour
Chilling time: 30 minutes

Crust:

Preheat oven to 375°. Crush in blender:

3 cups honey ginger snap crumbs (two 5-ounce packages)

Mix with:

½ cup plus 3 tablespoons melted butter
¼ teaspoon powdered ginger
1½ tablespoons honey

Press crumb mixture evenly in the bottom of a 9-inch

springform pan up to ¾ height of pan. Bake crust at 375°
for 8-10 minutes.

Filling:

Preheat oven to 400°. Beat until light and fluffy:

8 ounces cream cheese (room temperature)

Beat in, one at a time:

2 eggs
1 egg yolk

Stir in:

2 cups pumpkin purée
½ cup plus 2 tablespoons maple syrup
1 tablespoon cinnamon
½ teaspoon ground ginger
¼ teaspoon ground cloves
¼ teaspoon allspice
¼ teaspoon almond extract (optional)

Pour filling into crust and bake at 400° for 10 minutes.
Reduce heat to 325° and bake for 30 more minutes or
until center is barely set. Turn off oven and leave in
oven for 1 hour. Spread top of cheesecake with a mixture
of:

1½ cups sour cream
2 tablespoons maple syrup

Chill before serving.

Honey-
Butter Cream Icing

Preparation time: 10 minutes

Cream in large bowl:
12-14 tablespoons unsalted butter
⅔-¾ cup honey

Add:
pinch of salt
3-4 teaspoons vanilla

Sift in:
1 cup non-instant milk powder

Add and beat until fluffy:
1 tablespoon half and half (or more, if needed for desired consistency)

Variations:
1. Omit half and half and add:
freshly squeezed lemon or orange juice, and rind

2. Omit honey and use:
jam or jelly, to taste

Chocolate Sauce

Makes: 1 1/4 cups
or 12-14 servings

Delicious on ice cream, pound cake, dessert crêpes.

Preparation time: 12 minutes

Place in a small saucepan over low heat and whisk
until chocolate is melted and sauce thickens:

**3 ounces semi-sweet chocolate, chopped into small
pieces**
**1 ounce unsweetened chocolate, chopped into
small pieces**
³/₄ cup brown sugar
²/₃ cup half 'n half
2 teaspoons Grand Marnier (optional)
a pinch of salt

This sauce keeps well in the refrigerator for several
weeks.

Honey-Nut Sauce

Makes: 3½ cups

Preparation time: 20 minutes

Bring to a boil and boil for 1 minute:
2 cups honey

Add and bring to a boil again:
2 cubes butter, melted (½ pound)

Cook honey-butter mixture at a *very* low rolling boil for 10 minutes (as low as possible). After 10 minutes, remove from heat. Then add and mix well:
2 tablespoons cinnamon
2 teaspoons nutmeg
1½ teaspoons ground cloves
1 teaspoon ginger
1½ cups finely chopped walnuts

Serve as a sauce for crêpes or chilled as a topping for ice cream or yogurt.

Please note:

If overheated, sauce will harden like taffy. If sauce hardens, reheat over very low flame.

Beverages

Carob Froth

Makes: 4½ cups

Preparation time: 5 minutes

Combine in blender:

4 cups milk
6 rounded tablespoons raw carob powder
4 tablespoons honey
1 teaspoon cinnamon
1 teaspoon vanilla

Spicy Carob Milk

Makes: 3½ cups

Delicious cold or hot—almost a meal in itself.

Preparation time: 5-10 minutes

Combine in blender:

3 cups milk
1½ teaspoons molasses
1½ tablespoons honey
1 tablespoon toasted carob powder
½ teaspoon vanilla
¼ teaspoon powdered cardamon
½ teaspoon cinnamon
pinch of nutmeg
pinch of Postum

Variation:

When served cold, blend in:

1 banana

Lhassi

Makes: approximately 3 cups

Preparation time: 8 minutes

This sweet, refreshing drink is simple to make, and is traditionally served with Indian food. The charm of the drink is the subtle balance of sweet and sour.

The recipe below is a guideline only. The proportions will vary, depending on how thick or tart the yogurt is. Adjust them to suit your taste.

Blend in blender:
   1 cup yogurt
   2 cups cold water
   $^1/_3$ cup sugar
   4 ice cubes
   **optional: a few drops rosewater or $^1/_8$ teaspoon
      cardamom**

Serve well chilled.

Fresh Lime Soda

Makes: nearly 1^1/$_2$ quarts

A refreshing drink from India. Perfect for a hot day.

Preparation time: 10 minutes

Mix in a pitcher:
^{3}/$_4$ cup fresh squeezed lime juice (about 6 limes)
^{3}/$_4$-1 cup honey syrup* or to taste
4 cups club soda or sparkling mineral water

Serve chilled or over ice. Garnish with a slice of lime or sprig of mint.

*To help honey mix with cold drinks, make the honey syrup by mixing:
^{1}/$_2$ cup light honey (We use white clover honey.)
^{1}/$_2$ cup boiling water

Stir until honey liquifies.

Spicy Mandarin Orange Tea

Makes: 8 cups

Preparation time: 15 minutes

Bring to a boil:
**4 cups water
2-inch stick cinnamon
5 whole cloves
5 whole cardamom pods**

Turn off heat and add:
8 bags mandarin orange spice tea

Cover and let steep for 5 minutes. Remove tea bags
and add:
**4 cups apple juice
$^1/_2$ cup orange juice**

Heat and serve, garnished with:
slice of orange or lemon

Red Zinger Apple Punch   Makes: 3 quarts

Preparation time: 5-8 minutes

Steep for 5 minutes:
   8 cups boiling water
   8 bags Red Zinger tea

Remove tea bags and stir in:
   ½ cup honey

Then add:
   1 quart unsweetened apple juice
   juice and pulp of 2 limes (do not strain)

Garnish with:
   fresh mint leaves

Serve hot or cold.

Apple-Red Zinger Iced Tea   Makes: 2 quarts

Preparation time: 15 minutes
Chilling time: 1 to 2 hours

Let steep for 5 minutes:
   4 cups boiling water
   8 bags Red Zinger tea

Remove tea bags, pour tea into a 2½-quart pitcher, and stir in:
   2 tablespoons honey

When honey is completely dissolved, add:
3 cups apple juice
1 cup cold water
2 teaspoons lime juice

Refrigerate. Serve over ice and garnish with:
slice of lemon or lime

North African
Iced Mint Tea   Makes: 1 quart

A favorite on a warm summer evening.

Preparation time: 15 minutes
Chilling time: 1-2 hours

Let steep for 5 minutes:
4 cups boiling water
6 peppermint tea bags

Remove tea bags and add:
6 tablespoons honey (¼ cup plus 2 tablespoons)
1 tablespoon plus 2 teaspoons fresh lime juice
(1-2 limes)

Refrigerate for 1-2 hours. Serve over ice and garnish with:
slice of lemon or lime

To cool more quickly, use only 3 cups of boiling water and add 1 cup of cold water before adding ice.

Tropical Cooler

Makes: 2½ cups

Preparation time: 5-10 minutes

Combine in blender:

6 tablespoons papaya juice concentrate (3 ounces)
6 tablespoons pineapple-coconut juice (3 ounces)
¾ cup freshly squeezed orange juice (2-3 oranges)
2 ice cubes
1¼ cups water or, to taste

Serve over ice. Garnish with:

sprig of mint

Variation:

Before blending, add:

1 scoop of honey-vanilla ice cream

Honey-Lemonade

Preparation time: 10-15 minutes
Chilling time: 1-2 hours

Heat in small pan over medium heat until honey dissolves:

1 cup water
¼ cup honey

Mix together in pitcher:

honey-water mixture
4 cups cold water
¾ cup freshly squeezed lemon juice (3-4 lemons)

Add:

5 strips lemon rind
1 medium orange, thinly sliced

Refrigerate for 1-2 hours. Remove lemon rind and orange slices before serving.

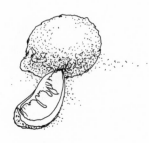

This & That

A Few Breakfast Ideas

Millet Pudding

Serves: 8

Preparation time: 40-45 minutes

In a large saucepan, sauté over medium heat for a few minutes until millet begins to toast (about 8 minutes), stirring frequently:

2 tablespoons safflower oil
2 tablespoons butter
2 cups millet

Add and bring to a boil:

5 cups water
2 sticks cinnamon
16 whole cloves
¼ teaspoon ground cardamon
½ teaspoon ground coriander
1½ cups (packed) chopped dates or date pieces
½ cup honey (optional)

Reduce heat, cover and simmer for 25 minutes or until water is absorbed. Add and stir in:

4 cups milk

Continue simmering very gently, stirring frequently until milk is absorbed and mixture is thick and creamy (about 20-30 minutes). Serve hot or cold. If desired add cream or milk.

Oatmeal Supreme

Serves: 8

Preparation time: 20 minutes

Combine in large saucepan and bring to a boil:
5 cups water
1½ teaspoons coriander
⅛ teaspoon ground cloves
¼ teaspoon powdered ginger
¾ teaspoon cinnamon

After water and spices come to a boil, add:
3¼ cups rolled oats
½ cup raw sunflower seeds
2 cups milk
2 cups grated apples
1 teaspoon vanilla
1 tablespoon fresh lemon juice

Cook over low heat until thickened. Top with honey and additional milk if desired.

Variation:

To every 2 cups of water add and purée in blender:
1 banana

Cook oatmeal in this "banana milk".

Apple Muesli

Serves: 6-8

Preparation time: 35 minutes
Soaking time: overnight

Soak in large bowl for 2-3 hours:
¾ cup rolled oats
1½ cups water

Drain off excess water. Add:
juice of 3 large lemons
¼ cup honey
½ cup cream

Then quickly add, stirring immediately to prevent apples from browning:
8 large apples, peeled, cored and grated (red delicious work best)

Stir mixture thoroughly and refrigerate overnight. Before serving, stir in:
4 large ripe bananas, mashed with a fork

Add:
1 teaspoon cinnamon
¼ teaspoon nutmeg
¼ teaspoon coriander
1 teaspoon lemon rind
1 cup ground almonds or more, to taste
raisins or currants, to taste

Variations:
1. Serve with:
sliced bananas

2. For a grainier mixture, increase the proportion of oats.

Appetizers and Snacks

Cheese Crackers

Makes: 20-25

Delicious, crisp, and flaky.

Preparation time: 15 minutes
Baking time: 6-8 minutes

Preheat oven to 475°. Mix together in medium bowl:

$1/4$ cup soft butter
**1 cup grated sharp cheddar cheese (about 1/4
    pound)**
$3/4$-1 teaspoon tamari

Stir in and work with fingers until well blended:

$3/4$ cup whole wheat pastry flour
pinch of onion powder
pinch of chile powder
pinch of curry powder
**optional: $1/2$-1 teaspoon water, if needed to hold
    mixture together**

Roll mixture until $1/4$ inch thick on an oiled cookie sheet. Prick with a fork and cut into squares. Bake at 475° for 6-8 minutes, until a rich golden brown.

Tofu-Chile Cheese Squares

Serves: 5-6

Rich and cheesy.

Preparation time: 30 minutes
Baking time: 30-35 minutes

Preheat oven to 350°. In blender, purée in 2 or 3 batches
until smooth and pour into large bowl:

3 eggs
¾ pound tofu
½ teaspoon salt

Stir in:

1 pound cheddar cheese, grated
one 7-ounce can green Ortega chiles, chopped

Spread mixture evenly in a buttered 8-inch square pan
and sprinkle with:

1½ tablespoons finely grated fresh Parmesan cheese
paprika

Bake at 350° for 30-35 minutes. Can be a main dish or
appetizer.

Mexican Cheese Melts

Serves: 6-8

A do-ahead time-saver.

Preparation time: 10 minutes

Mix together in medium bowl:

4 ounces sharp cheddar cheese, grated
4 ounces mozzarella cheese, grated
1 small can chopped Ortega green chiles
1 large clove garlic, crushed
1 cup mayonnaise

Spread mixture on sliced sour dough bread. Place slices on cookie sheet and freeze until firm. When frozen, stack slices and store in plastic bag in freezer. Take out as needed. Do not defrost. Bake at 325° until cheese is melted. Excellent for brunches, lunches, and, on cocktail rounds, as an appetizer.

English Muffin Melts

Serves: 6-8

Preparation time: 15 minutes

Preheat oven to 400°. Mix together in medium bowl:

one 4-ounce can chopped black olives, drained
2 tablespoons finely chopped onion
1 teaspoon curry powder
½ teaspoon garlic powder
1 cup grated sharp cheddar cheese
2 tablespoons mayonnaise

Spread on English muffins and bake at 400° until cheese melts. Cut muffins into quarters and serve as appetizers. Mixture can also be spread on crackers and served cold.

Marinated Mushrooms   Makes: 1½ cups, drained

Preparation time: 12-15 minutes
Marinating time: 24 hours

Combine in small bowl and whisk together:
½ cup apple cider vinegar
½ cup olive oil
2 teaspoons basil
2 teaspoons marjoram
2 teaspoons yellow mustard seeds
1 teaspoon onion salt
¼ teaspoon garlic powder
2-3 dashes Worcestershire sauce
pinch of cayenne

Pour mixture over:
**3 cups (packed) small button mushrooms or thickly
    sliced larger mushrooms (approximately ½
    pound)**

Refrigerate mushrooms for 24 hours, stirring occasionally.
Drain and serve as an appetizer, or leave in marinade and
serve on crisp lettuce leaves as a salad.

Marinated Tofu

Makes: 5 cups, drained

Preparation time: 20-25 minutes
Marinating time: 1 hour

Combine in blender:

1 cup apple cider vinegar or fresh lemon juice
1 cup tamari
1 1/2 cups safflower or other light tasting oil
1 teaspoon <u>toasted</u> sesame oil
1 teaspoon grated fresh ginger
2 teaspoons basil
6 large cloves garlic, peeled

Pour mixture over:

1 1/2 pounds firm tofu, cut into small cubes

Marinate tofu 1 hour, stirring occasionally.
Serve as a main dish, side dish, or as an appetizer.
The marinade can be re-used for another batch of tofu.

Herbed Croutons

Makes: 2½ cups

Preparation time: 30 minutes

Crush in mortar:
1 tablespoon thyme
1 teaspoon basil
1 teaspoon paprika
½ teaspoon oregano
2 rounded tablespoons minced fresh parsley
1 teaspoon onion powder
3 large cloves garlic

Combine herb mixture with:
1 cube butter, melted (¼ pound)

Brush mixture onto both sides of:
9-10 slices whole wheat bread

Cut bread into cubes and toast in a dry skillet for
10-15 minutes, or until crisp and browned. Watch
closely so that croutons don't burn. They can be frozen
for later use.

Popcorn Deluxe

Makes: 1 batch in hot air popper

Preparation time: 7 minutes

Pop in hot air popper:
¹/₂ cup popcorn

Add and mix well in a large bowl:
6 tablespoons melted butter

Sprinkle popcorn with a mixture of:
¹/₄ cup flaked nutritional yeast
2-3 teaspoons curry powder

Add:
salt, to taste

Variations

I.   Add to popped corn:
6 tablespoons melted butter
¹/₄cup flaked nutritional yeast
¹/₄ teaspoon garlic powder or granules
cayenne to taste
4 teaspoons fresh lemon juice
salt, if desired

II.   Add to popped corn:
4 dried tomatoes, powdered in blender
1 tablespoon oregano
¹/₄ cup dried parmesan
salt to taste

Glossary

MOST OF THE INGREDIENTS we use in *Simply Vegetarian!* are available in supermarkets. The following items, which we use in some recipes, are more readily available in health food stores.

Agar flakes
> A gelatin made from sea weed

Arrowroot
> A natural thickening agent

Basmati rice
> A long grain scented rice which exudes a perfumed nutty aroma. Traditionally a favorite in North Indian regional cuisines, well-aged basmati rice is considered the finest rice in the world by many cooks.

Bulgur wheat
> A pre-cooked and dried cracked wheat

Carob powder
> A chocolate substitute

Chappati
> Unleavened bread made with wheat flour

Garbanzo flour
> Made from garbanzo beans

Miso
> A thick paste made from fermented soybeans and wheat

Nutritional yeast
> A non-leavening yeast, high in B-vitamins

Potato flour
> Made of pure potato without the skins. It has a granulated consistency and blends more easily with liquid than other flours.

Potato starch
>   Of a finer consistency than potato flour, similar to corn starch

Sesame spaghetti
>   Pasta that includes some sesame flour

Stripples
>   Brand name for a bacon substitute made from soybeans

Tahini
>   A paste made from sesame seeds

Tamari
>   A type of soy sauce

Tofu
>   Soybean curd

Vegit
>   Brand name for a vegetable seasoning

Whole wheat flour
>   Flour ground using the whole wheat berry including the bran and germ

Whole wheat pastry flour
>   Flour ground from soft wheat which is low in gluten to give a lighter texture to cakes, biscuits and pastries.

Index

Also from DAWN Publications:

Health and Fitness

The Main Ingredients of Health and Happiness Susan Smith Jones, Ph.D., introduces the reader to a wide range of choices which help bring the body, mind and spirit to higher levels of wellness (juices to exercise to meditation to natural hygiene). *$14.95 paper*

Quest for Life: A Guidebook for People with Life-Threatening Illness A sound, practical, and comprehensive guide to dealing with all the aspects of having a life-threatening illness. *Petrea King $12.95 paper*

Nature Awareness and Children's

A Walk in the Rainforest Introduces children to the fascinating world of the tropical rainforest. 26 delightful illustrations and text by 15-year old Kristin Joy Pratt. *Ages 3-10 $7.95 soft, $16.95 hard*

A Swim through the Sea Follow Seamore the Seahorse as we explore the world of the ocean. 26 beautiful illustrations and text by 17-year-old Kristin Joy Pratt. *Teachers's Choice Award, 1996.* Ages 3-10 *$7.95 soft, $16.95 hard*

A Fly in the Sky Thethird in Kristin Joy Pratt's nature trilogy. A joyful exploration of birds, insects, and other animals of the air. *Ages 3-10. $7.95 paper, $16.95 hard*

Discover the Seasons Rich illustrations and sensitive poetry introduce the younger child to the changing seasons: *celebration* for spring, *learning* for summer, *work* for fall and *rest* for winter. Followed by hands-on activities and recipes. *Diane Iverson Ages 3-10 $9.95 paper*

Grandpa's Garden Grandpa and grandchild lovingly share their deepest feelings and talk of life's lessons, as they work side by side in his garden. *Shea Darian Illustrated by Karlyn Holman Ages 4-10 $7.95 paper*

Sharing Nature with Children The classic nature awareness guidebook used by parents, educators, and naturalists everywhere. *Joseph Cornell $7.95 paper*

Listening to Nature A beautiful gift book featuring, for each day of the month, inspiring quotes from the likes of Muir and Thoreau. 41 stunning photographs by Sierra Club Calendar veteran John Hendrickson. *Joseph Cornell $12.95 paper*

DAWN PUBLICATIONS

For a complete listing of our products, send for a Dawn Publications catalog.

Quantity	Item	Price
_____	*Simply Vegetarian!* _____	$11.95 ____
_____	_____	_____
_____	_____	_____
_____	_____	_____
_____	_____	_____
_____	_____	_____
_____	_____	_____
_____	_____	_____

7.25% tax in California _____

Shipping: $4.25 for 1 or 2 items; $5.25 for more _____

TOTAL _____

Please send payment and order to:
DAWN Publications
14618 Tyler Foote Road
Nevada City, CA 95959
Call toll free (800)545-7475

Name _____

Address _____

City/State/Zip_____

Phone _____

Please charge to my credit card number_____

☐ VISA ☐ MasterCard   Exp. Date _____

ORDER FORM

Comments

We are always interested in getting your comments on our recipes that you have tried. Or, if you have any other suggestions, please don't hesitate to drop us a line. We'd love to hear from you.

Joy to you,

Nancy Mair and Susan Rinzler,
Editors

c/o *Simply Vegetarian!*
DAWN Publications
14618 Tyler Foote Road
Nevada City, CA 95959